Happy Birthday,
we love you
Antoinette + Cristiane

November 2 2023

Yoga of Liberation

A heart-based path to spiritual awakening

Craig Holliday

Yoga of Liberation
A heart-based path to spiritual awakening

Craig Holliday
www.craigholliday.com

Library of Congress Cataloging-in-Publication Data
Printed in the United States of America
First Edition: November 2020
ISBN-13: 978-0-9911307-1-9
Editor: Suzanne Winters

Disclaimer: This publication is designed to provide accurate and personal experience information regarding the subject matter covered. It is sold with the understanding that the author, contributors, and publisher are not engaged in rendering counseling or other professional services through this publication. If counseling advice or other expert assistance is required, the services of a competent professional person should be sought out.

Copyright © 2020 Craig Holliday. All rights reserved. Except as permitted under U.S. Copyright Act of 1976, no part of this publication may be reproduced, distributed, or transmitted in any form or by any means, or stored in a database or retrieval system, without the prior written permission of the publisher.

Acknowledgments

To my family, each one of you, thank you sincerely for all the love and continued support. Thank you for challenging me to be a greater father, for parenthood is a true test of character and demands that we walk the talk, embody the truth, and learn unconditional love—off the meditation cushion. Thank you, Suzanne, for the countless hours of editing this book and bringing it print. Your tireless support and encouragement made this possible.

To all of my teachers, thank you. I bow before you. To David, my root teacher, for patiently and sternly—but compassionately—showing me a much greater world beyond ego. Thank you for spending two decades of your life showing me the way of Mastery. I strive to walk fully in your footsteps one day. To Adyashanti, Ammachi, Lama Tsultrim, Eli Jaxon Bear, and all my teachers in this lifetime, I bow before Thee. Thank you for illuminating the path and sharing with me the awakened experience. To Sri Aurobindo, Buddha, and Christ, I continue to open my heart to you, and I continue to pray that You will lead and guide me in this world.

Dear readers, please know that anything you gain from this work is not mine, but rather it is a gift that was given to me by my teachers. This is how the dharma is spread: from one open heart to another. In a sense, everything of value in this book is all plagiarized from the Masters. I am an ordinary man with an ordinary mind—yet something extraordinary was given to me. This gift, I attempt to share with you.

~ *Craig Holliday*

Table of Contents

To all who are on the Path, my heart is with you.

Chapter One

Yoga of Liberation

Ever being Buddha, ever becoming Buddha.

AT THE HEART OF ALL GREAT SPIRITUAL PATHS WAS A YOGI—one who discovered and lived from the direct experience of the Divine in their mind, heart, and soul. All of us have this capacity to live in union with our highest nature—to live in union from the ineffable presence of our hearts.

The spiritual path can be summed up in one movement: from darkness toward the light, from unconsciousness to a greater Consciousness. This movement encompasses the transition from experiencing ourselves as fear-based human animals to the direct recognition that we are Divine beings whose expression is Love, Truth, and Beauty in the world. This path is an ongoing evolution from being narrow-minded and self-centered toward a greater and continuously expanding openness and inclusion of every aspect of life. This spiritual path is not simply about being open and compassionate when we are practicing yoga or meditation. It is the total embrace of ourselves—the good, the bad and the ugly—as well as the total embrace of life in all Her manifestations. It is through this path that we discover a complete non-division within ourselves so thorough, that we become fully and incomprehensibly one with the Divine.

The Yoga of Liberation is a movement from being inwardly divided, lost, and confused by our fragmented egoic nature to becoming whole, integrated, and unified with our inherent *divine essence,* which is Love,

Truth, and Beauty. It is a movement toward alignment and oneness with the Divine, both in our absolute nature, which we experience in times of meditation and union with the Divine, as well as in our everyday lives while we are running around at work or raising our children. True yoga is not a spiritual practice—it is a way of life where there is no separation between the depth of what we are and how we live. To live in this way requires a deep and ongoing surrender to something much greater than our habitual and conditioned egoic minds.

From an absolute perspective, we are already fully one with God, both in our essential nature and in our humanity. We were made by Life and we are *Life Itself* in human form. There is no way we could step out of our essential nature. There is nothing we could do that God Herself did not allow, create, or put in motion. All is God, all is one. As human beings, we have every layer of creation within us—from the highest manifestations to the lowest. This is why, within the course of a single day, we can express both the compassion of the Buddha as well as anger or rage. God, Life, the Universe, and us are all one. And all of us together, as one, are continuously evolving. At this time in history, our collective evolution requires that we either take the higher path toward God consciousness—through evolving out of our animal nature and stepping into our Higher Divine nature of Love and Truth—or suffer the fate of the dinosaurs and cease to exist.

From a relative and humble perspective, we are all a work in progress. Most of us live in a state of chaos, inner division, and suffering which would be hard to describe as "Divine." But despite our confusing and chaotic lives, this is an evolutionary world, and we are all evolving toward a greater and greater manifestation of Divinity. From this place of understanding and acknowledging the evolutionary context of life, we each must ask ourselves, "Am I evolving consciously?" If not, our evolution as human beings will be unconscious and painstakingly slow—one of turmoil, pain, and suffering. We will suffer, those around us will suffer, and perhaps even the fate of the planet will suffer.

Yoga of Liberation is a path to wake up to our absolute nature of Divinity, to come to know that we are Divine in the deepest essence of ourselves, and to allow this Divinity to become manifest in our humanity. It is also the recognition that our very humanity is Divine— we were made in the image and likeness of God. This is the great paradox of life: we are both already human *and Divine*, one and the same movement of God, here in form. We are Buddhas and are always becoming Buddhas. In our nature and essence we are absolutely Divine, and also in our nature and humanity we are ever evolving out of the animal kingdom and into the Divine Kingdom. This book is an invitation into this paradox to realize our innate Divinity through embracing and embodying our full humanity in an evolutionary context.

In the heart of the yogic teachings and in all of the great wisdom traditions is this invitation to know ourselves as Divine, as well as instruction on how to live fully in alignment with the truth that we are one with all of existence. Unfortunately, most modern day yoga taught and practiced today in the West puts emphasis on yoga as being just a form of exercise. True yoga is a doorway to Liberation from our egoic identification and to the discovery of our inherent Divinity that arises when we step beyond our egoic conditioning and embody our Divine essence. The real power of Yoga is to awaken us to the radiance of our true nature. After all, deeper than simply desiring to have a great "yoga body," what we sincerely desire is *to know ourselves as Divine in every aspect of our being.*

Until we know this direct experience of Divinity as our very nature, we will be sorely disappointed in our spiritual practices and everyday lives—nothing will satisfy. This inherent dissatisfaction is why we never give up the path and continue walking toward the light. It is also this inherent dissatisfaction that is the very mind of God, expressing Her agenda for evolution, for God *is* evolution. Beyond being vast, empty, spacious, peace, love, and light, She is also the very movement of Evolution—of Light giving birth to form.

The direct experience of radiance is what attracts us to the spiritual path. We experience the power and grace of divinity anytime we practice yoga or meditation. As we practice, we are getting out of our heads and opening into the experience of our subtle body. As we do so, we naturally unhook from the compulsive and neurotic identification with our minds and step into something beyond mind; beyond both thought and ego. That which we are stepping into is our inherent aliveness—it is the direct experience of our Divinity.

This book is a compilation of reflections and teachings on the disciplines, attitudes, and perspectives necessary to know and directly experience ourselves as this continuously evolving radiance; a radiance which is available to us all, for it is our very nature. Our experience of ourselves in this incomprehensible way is not dependent upon knowledge of yogic teachings and methods, nor does it matter if we are Buddhist, Christian, Jewish, or Muslim.

To know our radiance, we do not have to be a monk or scholar. We only have to possess a sincere desire to know what we truly are in the depth of our being. Unfortunately, many of us think that the spiritual path is a path of knowledge which focuses on the study of scriptures and sutras alone. This mental emphasis of the spiritual path gives rise to the perspective that we become enlightened in our minds. This is an innocent arrogance on our part. We do not need to have studied Buddhism and be able to speak fluently about the sutras. It is not necessary that we read hundreds of religious texts in order to become Awake. We may find ourselves asking, what is the point of our study if our direct experience is not one of vastness and compassion? Fortunately, everything we need is in our very hearts. No sutra or book (not even this one) can give us the direct experience of ourselves. The teachings offered here are simply invitations into your own heart space to experience for yourself what you truly are.

The direct incomprehensible experience of ourselves as Divine is our birthright. It is available to each and every one of us, no matter what our past is or which religion we come from. Jesus very clearly found this truth within himself when he stated, "I am the son of God" and quickly forgave everyone in his company. Yet this truth is not reserved for one man, but is true for all of us. We are all Divine. Jesus did not say, "I am the one and only," or "I am and you are not." He simply tried to remind us, through His presence, that we are all the sons and daughters of God. It was the religious institutions which came along later that tried to trademark this truth and created great suffering as a result. But we do not have to sheepishly follow the politics of these institutions. We can come into our hearts and see for ourselves that we are Divine. This is my invitation to you—to directly experience your true Divine nature.

This book has very little to do with particular yogic asanas, spiritual rituals, or complicated meditation practices. In most chapters I offer some basic guidance to develop the practices discussed. This book is intended to be a practical, down-to-earth guide to the attitudes and perspectives necessary to truly discover Yoga—union with God. It is through this absolute union with our Divinity and the embodiment of this Divinity in our everyday lives that we attain liberation from our egoic nature.

Liberation is the goal of yoga: to know and directly experience oneself as Divine and to live this Divinity in our everyday lives. As we do so our world grows, evolving out of darkness and into a greater expression of consciousness. It is not that liberation is a place we get to, but rather an expression of total alignment with our Divinity, including our ever-evolving Divinity.

Again, we are all Buddhas and ever becoming Buddhas. This is the paradox of God, evolving into greater manifestations of Herself, in the form of you and I. At their core, all spiritual practices, asanas, meditations, and rituals are meant to take us somewhere beyond our narrow everyday view. Where we are taken, though, is ultimately dependent upon our intention. This book is about aligning with the clear intention of liberation from our egoic self through the continual surrender into our Divine Self. This is the primary movement which is at the heart of all yogic teachings and any true spiritual teaching.

This powerful intention has, at its foundation, the following spiritual qualities and attitudes: sincerity, valuing truth above all else, honesty, humility, compassion, peacefulness, concentration, diligence, discipline, knowledge, unity, oneness, and reverence for the evolutionary context, which is God. These attitudes and qualities of self are not something we create, but rather something to be discovered within us, and can only truly be known through directly experiencing the truth of oneself.

Our work is to first align our heart, mind, attention, and energy with these intentions and then allow these intentions to fuel our practices. The actual form of practice does not make a difference. Whether your practice includes asanas, contemplation, meditation, prayer, dance, ritual, or inquiry—you must choose which resonates with your heart. What makes the difference is that you are sincere in your desire to find the truth of yourself.

What follows is a series of reflections, inquiry questions, contemplations, and meditations which invoke the direct experience of Yoga—the direct experience of union with God, with Life Itself.

This invitation to experience ourselves as Divine is not something we simply reserve for the time we set aside each day to practice. This invitation is to know ourselves as Divine in every aspect of our lives— to know this Divinity as we change our baby's diapers, speak with our boss, stand on a mountaintop, or practice on our meditation cushions. What we ultimately discover at the end of the spiritual path is that nothing is outside of or apart from the Divine. This book is an invitation to discover this in every moment of our lives.

Chapter Two

The Attitude of Liberation

THERE IS A VERY MYSTERIOUS GRACE WHICH BRINGS us all to the spiritual path. Whether our sincere interest in spirituality arose after a tragedy, such as the death of a loved one or a divorce, or because we simply heard the word *awakening* and something inside us came alive, this force moves our heart toward God. There are many ways in which can we find ourselves deeply contemplating the meaning of life. But there is something that cannot be denied—the desire for Truth, Love and Beauty will ultimately propel us into a life with greater meaning, purpose, and connection.

For most of us, we are here because our lives have collided with the Dharma—with a greater Reality which we cannot ignore. And once we heard the nourishing words of the Dharma, our hearts lit up and we knew that we were on our way home to our true self, to the self which is free of our egoic drama, free of our neurotic stories, and free of our painful defenses and attachments. It is in this newfound freedom that we discover an aliveness which is connected to the goodness of all of life; we discover a Beauty which has no end, a Freedom larger than the sky *as our very own nature.* Yet most of us only glimpse this Beauty and Freedom and then shy away from it. We are too frightened by Its immensity to dive fully into this Divinity and let it consume us. For most of us, this potential to live as our highest self eludes us because we are frightened of *giving up what we know* and *what we have known ourselves to be.* If we are ruled by fear then soon this glimpse, which was handed to us by Grace, becomes overshadowed by our unconsciousness and falls out of our reach. In this moment of fear, we again become easily confused by our minds because we have no discipline, courage, or wisdom, and so fall painfully short of what is possible for us in this amazing world of spirit. To realize this greater potential of spiritual awakening, we have to first have a sense of faith that living in our full Divinity is possible for us in this lifetime, as well as the conviction to give all of ourselves to this vision or *to die trying*.

As a teacher, one of my greatest challenges is conveying to individuals that they are worthy of their own Divinity—that within each and every soul is a vast spacious presence and a loving heart which can fully manifest itself in us and as Us, and that we are strong enough to walk the spiritual path to realization. Unfortunately, many of us are wounded, lacking confidence, and struggling too much to claim this inner Divinity. Yet, to walk forward on the path, we must at least have faith that *what we are is Divine* and that we can realize this Divinity in this lifetime. Without this sense of faith and commitment to the greater discovery of what we truly are, our spiritual path will be lacking power and drive. It is hard to go forward if we never believe that we are worthy of the direction in which we are headed.

There are many attitudes and ways of being that we must cultivate and nourish, both to walk forward and not become so easily lost in Samsara (the realms of our unconscious nature). To truly give ourselves to the path is not a light endeavor. It takes everything within us to truly discover the depth of what we are. These words are an invitation to embark fully on the path.

The primary intention we must commit ourselves to on this path of liberation is to know and be oneself fully. We must be willing to soundly voice, "I am an incarnation of the Divine and I will discover and embody this fully in this lifetime!" When we make a commitment like this, our hearts wake up. We know for the first time what our lives are about. If we enthusiastically state out loud, "I am committed to knowing myself as Divine in every aspect of my being!" we discover that our commitment comes with a force, a power, and a challenge. We will soon come to know that our lives are no longer about our old egoic way of being. We may even become somewhat frightened because we know that we will be giving up our old habitual way of being. When we commit ourselves in this way, we choose to walk against the grain of the collective unconsciousness. However, we do not have to do this alone. Millions of spiritual aspirants who have gone before us on this path all knew this fear. Because we have made our commitment from our heart space, we choose to courageously walk forward in truth. We choose to walk into the unknown. This marks the true beginning of our path. This commitment is non-negotiable and fully necessary if we are going to truly go forward on the path of liberation.

At the heart of all spiritual teachings is this truth, that we are one with the Divine, with Life, with God, with Atman, with Buddha Nature, with Christ... the names do not really matter. What matters is the realization that we are one with Divinity. The force that comes forward when we speak this out loud is our heart waking up to itself and saying yes, this is true. Contrary to this, we may also notice our egoic mind simultaneously coming forward and giving us a list of reasons why we are not divine.

And so follows our challenge: Do we listen to our heart and heal and transform our egoic minds through the practice of Love, clear seeing, and compassion? Or do we listen to the same old story which repeats itself over and over in our minds? If we take the challenge of choosing to live in the wisdom of our hearts, we will be asked to surrender our arrogant and neurotic minds again and again, until they come into full

17

alignment with the beauty and wisdom of our hearts. To go forward, we must begin with a sense of faith that what we are in our core is Divine. This faith begins with us becoming silent and directly experiencing the warmth and aliveness of our presence, which lies in the center of our heart. This direct experience of our Divinity aligned with a commitment to know this Beauty in every aspect of our lives is our challenge. If we make this commitment to ourselves, we consciously and wholeheartedly step onto the path of liberation.

What is it that we are liberated from? We are liberated from our own arrogant, neurotic, self-serving, habitual egoic tendencies. We are liberated from our egoic hopes and fears, cravings and compulsions, past and future, and from the feeling of separation that comes from not knowing who we truly are. We are liberated from being guarded, needy, and aggressive or passive. When we are free of these unconscious mind states, what we discover is our own original nature: vibrant, alive, happy, and ever-expanding Life.

Many of us though are not so interested in liberation and instead choose to "lead lives of quiet desperation," as Henry David Thoreau put it. Most of us on the spiritual path only temporarily glimpse our Divinity and then a few moments later find ourselves once again lost in our current dramas, internal fantasies, or fears. In order to truly discover our True selves, we must make this commitment above all else to know ourselves as Divine. This challenge is for the bold, for those who have already tried to find happiness in relationships, careers, material possessions, travel, drugs, and alcohol, but have found no salvation. The truth is that there is no salvation outside of our Self. At the end of all our seeking and grasping outside of ourselves, it begins to dawn upon us that the only place that we have not looked, is within our very hearts. When we have exhausted all other measures, we find that all true happiness and contentment come from the discovery of our innate Divinity.

Saints and sages have reminded us of this since the beginning of time. But because we have been born with egoic minds which seem to be endlessly lost and searching outside of ourselves, we never seem to discover this truth; we may only glimpse it. For us to truly live as the Beauty of our very own hearts, we must make a commitment to love ourselves enough to dedicate our lives to the path before us. If we do not make this commitment our absolute priority, our busy and neurotic minds will steer us in ten thousand different directions. We will slowly evolve on the path at the rate of the collective unconsciousness, and we can observe from the nightly news that our world is barely surviving. If we desire true awakening and make this commitment, we step into our Truth and our power, and from this place we consciously walk forward.

If we want to be free, the primary attitude that we must choose to cultivate and embody is:

Divinity is my nature.

With this vision in our hearts, we commit to making this vision a reality. It is here that we are called to action. We choose to take the time each day to silently go inward and discover this truth again and again until we experience this divinity in every cell of our being. We start this journey with a faith that "I am Divine" and watch as our faith quickly turns into knowledge through directly experiencing ourselves as Divine.

The following chapters will offer a series of teachings on stepping out of our habitual minds and into the Presence which is here in every moment. We must remember, though, that it is not the particular practice that is important, but rather the space from which we practice. The individual practices themselves do not make a difference; whether it is an asana practice, meditation, or prayer, we must first unhook from our minds and come into the direct experience of God first and foremost if our practices are going to deeply move us.

With this greater perspective and connection to that which is Divine within us, we now experience that our practice is fueled by Grace. As we practice in this way, we free ourselves from our minds through surrendering to that which is greater than our limited egoic nature.

Practice: What is Holding You Back?

Contemplate what your priorities are in life and ask yourself the following questions:

- Do I want to truly wake up in this lifetime? Do I believe that this is possible?

- What are my conscious intentions for the spiritual path?

- What is holding me back from fully stepping onto the spiritual path?

- In what ways do I ignore my true nature or God?

- What habits, ideas, and beliefs hold me back from the recognition of my true nature?

- What disconnects me from my heart?

- What reconnects me to my essence?

Chapter Three

All is One: The Direct Experience of Oneness

MOST SPIRITUAL TRADITIONS, AT THEIR CORE, teach that "all is one" and that the concept of a separate egoic self is false. But for most of us living in the practical everyday world of career, children, marriage, and relationships, this teaching makes little to no sense and is quite contrary to our everyday experience. Because of this, we pay little attention to this teaching and inherent truth. However, if we quickly dismiss this teaching, we miss the whole focus of spirituality, which is to know ourselves as one with the Divine and with all of life. If we do take the time to sincerely investigate this profound teaching of the reality of oneness, it has the potential to radically reorient our everyday lives in unimaginably immense ways.

To open to the experience of oneness directly, we must investigate what it is within us that separates us from this direct experience of Reality. We must examine why we do not naturally live from the truth of our being. When we examine this question of identity, we begin to see that it is the experience of the egoic self which separates us from the greater experience of oneness and true nondual Reality. When we step out of our mental and emotional worlds and look at what is here, we see that what we are—awake awareness—and the internal movement of psychological forces, are two separate things. We see that the separate egoic self is made up of the psychological forces arising within us. These psychological forces defend us from danger (both real and imagined), attach to or pursue what we desire, and mentally and emotionally organize our experience of the world.

Our egoic self also includes all the conditioning we receive from our family, education, and culture, as well as our species and collective consciousness. This egoic force of separation and individuation is necessary because at the core of our being and experience we are *one with all of life* and in no way separate from all others. Our egoic nature is a force which arises within our consciousness to help us to function as a separate entity in this world so that we can experience life as an individual. Without an ego, we would be like a newborn baby living in undifferentiated oneness with our mother and environment.

Our egoic nature is not inherently good or bad, although most ancient spiritual teachings which arose out of monastic traditions did not value the full human experience, such as family, relationships, and careers. Instead, they denied the human experience and simply advised to transcend life. Therefore, these teachings focused on eliminating the human, including the ego, condemning them as obstacles of oneness. For example, Christianity views human beings as inherently sinful. Buddhism teaches us to ignore our body and sensory experiences in life. The Buddha himself walked out on his wife and children in the middle of the night to search for his own liberation. A notable critique that many mothers have shared with me over the years is that most spiritual teachings do not honor or connect with the unconditional loving nature that arises in the experience of being a parent, a fundamental aspect of being human. All of us have parents, and many of us are parents. And yet, since most of us are not living in a monastery or convent, we need a spiritual teaching that is inclusive of *all aspects of our human self.*

This false view—that we are inherently bad, sinful, or wrong—occurred because most spiritual traditions were trying to transcend life and, at that moment in history, did not have an understanding of developmental psychology. They did not understand the ego's place or function within us and in human life. Ultimately, the ego is a neutral force attempting to live a good and safe life. But at the core of the ego is a psychological program driven by fear and pleasure, and conditioned by our past experiences. As a result of our past conditioning, our egoic nature will range from relatively healthy and trusting of life to unhealthy, defensive, guarded, and aggressive. This inner experience is dependent upon our past conditioning, and the unconscious and habitual patterns that we developed in response to our past experiences.

This essential force of ego is a developmental and survival force. It is natural and necessary so that we individuate in this world and become independent from our mothers and environment. Without the arising of our egoic nature, we would never detach from our mother, which would make it difficult for us to develop beyond toddlerhood. This force of individuation protects us and helps us to organize reality so that we may function in this world. A newborn baby does not possess an ego and, as a result of this lack, cannot function or differentiate herself from her world. In a sense, a baby lives in undifferentiated oneness. This is why, whether we realize it or not, oneness is at the core of our experience. Our ego was created by the Intelligence of Oneness, of Life, so that we could experience individuality and ultimately realize oneness through the experience of an individual— this journey is what becomes the spiritual path. How else could oneness experience itself if not through a conscious individual?

Ironically, it is through having an ego and developing a healthy sense of individuality and then letting go of that very ego that we can truly realize that we are one with God, Life, and the Universe. The journey toward individuated oneness is very much like the journey to adulthood. As children, we had to journey through school adopting and then later letting go of the rules and collective consciousness of each school or grade so that we could move on to that which is greater. We had to let go of the rules of elementary school as we walked into middle school. But we do not let go of what was good that we learned in elementary school. The same is true with egoic learning, development and letting go; we keep what is good, healthy, and necessary, and let go of that which is unhelpful or obsolete. As children, we adopted the rules of the playground and middle school relationships only to learn from them, and thankfully, let them go later. A healthy ego learns and grows in the experience of love, compassion, truth, honesty, and integrity, while letting go of that which no longer serves us. It is these very qualities of unity which support the experience and expression of oneness within oneself and the world.

Because the ego is such a powerful and seductive force, most of us find it difficult to become aware of our egoic nature as simply an impersonal force of nature. In a similar way, as teenagers we often are very unaware of the hormones running through our body and unconsciously believe the accompanying thoughts and emotions that come with them. This dance of mind and ego continues unchecked for most of our lives. This egoic force is so seductively convincing because of the projected virtual reality of thoughts and emotions which it self-fabricates. As a result, many of us fail to realize that our ego is more like a movie projector than our true self. Just as a movie projector projects the film within it onto a screen, ego projects onto the screen of our mind a repetition of pain and pleasure drives, mixed with the historical conditioning of our past experiences.

Spiritual awakening begins when we see that ego is merely an elaborate projector and realize that what we actually are is the living presence which is here before, during, and after this egoic projection. True spiritual awakening is the realization that ego is not the truth of us—that what we are is far greater than simply an arising movement of drives, habits, and conditioning. What we are is the very awake aware space in which the dance of ego and life arise.

If we step back out of the movie theater of our mind and view ourselves from the space of awareness, we begin to see that these psychological forces are movements within us, *but are not us*. When we investigate this more extensively, we find that there is no thing or solid entity within us that we can truly call "me." We may find many patterns of thoughts, behaviors, and emotions, but ultimately we will see that our egoic nature is simply a group of patterns which have been given to us by life. Ego is simply a collection of psychological patterns and conditioning which has been handed down to us by our culture and ancestors. Yet, because we have spent our lives entranced by these forces and have taken them to be real, we unconsciously conclude that these forces are what we are. Because we have been conditioned to identify with our thoughts and emotions in such a strong way by our family, friends, and educational systems, we no longer question this movement within us. Therefore, we never see these movements as arising forces within us and instead identify with them as a "me."

Through our journey on the spiritual path, we begin to loosen our identification with this separate egoic self. We begin to discover that we are not our mind, that we can see and observe our mind, and therefore, what we are is greater than our mind. We begin to see that we are not our emotions; that our emotions arise *within the space of what we are*, and therefore, know that our emotions are not essentially what we are. Through this work of first observing our mind and emotions from a space of mindfulness, we discover a sense of space between what we are and what we have known ourselves to be for so long. Through this practice of mindfulness, we can begin to observe these patterns that arise within us and choose which to allow and which to dismiss. Through the act of mindfulness, we become empowered and free from our past conditioning.

Beyond the ability to witness our minds and emotional nature, there is also the potential for another great shift that we can make here. It is first through mindfulness that we choose to step out of our minds and egos and discover a sense of innate spaciousness; from this space we can observe what is arising within us. It is from this perspective that something quite powerful can occur if we then *choose to turn our awareness upon itself.* It is from this turning inward and *allowing awareness to become aware of itself* that we discover what we actually are.

Unfortunately, many of us on the spiritual path unconsciously stop at the practice of becoming aware of our thoughts and do not step into this next level of being. But when we choose to turn awareness upon itself, we find that what we are is this vast luminous Mystery. It is from this space of being—this great Mystery that we are—that we discover we are one with all of life. We discover that we are not some limited separate egoic identity called Craig, Amaya, or Jose. We discover that there is no end to our consciousness—that what we are is in no way limited by our egoic nature. We see that our egoic nature is simply an overlay of mind with no inherent power. It is through the spiritual path that we free ourselves from this prison of separate egoic identification and discover oneness, unity, and freedom. And soon our whole life experience begins to reorient in a profound way. To be clear, this is not a mental or intellectual realization or new philosophy which is attained within the egoic mind. This realization is *experienced directly beyond mind.* What one knows oneself to be in their direct experience is vast luminous freedom... not the thought of freedom or the memory of a past spiritual experience, but freedom itself, living and breathing in the form of *I.*

Discovering our true nature beyond egoic identification is the most important spiritual discovery on the path because this discovery dislodges the primary illusion from which we all suffer. Once we begin to dislodge this illusion from our consciousness, we begin to grow, learn, and evolve at an exponential rate. This is because, for the first time in our lives, our egoic nature is not getting in the way and painting our reality and experience of life. It is no longer constantly separating us from our hearts, from God, from Life, and from each other. When we discover that who and what we are is one with all of life, we begin to experience that oneness, compassion, and kindness are inseparable. We find that we do not have to effort so intensely to be kind or compassionate, for compassion becomes our nature. What we discover is that it is much easier to be kind and compassionate to our "enemies" because we see that we are not separate from them. It is easier for us to live our Yoga, Buddhism, or Christianity because everywhere we look we see God and Buddha nature. Not only is it simpler to be less self-centered, it also becomes natural to see and meet all of life from this space of Unity. To see life otherwise would create division and suffering within us, and in turn, within the world.

When we discover that we are not our egos, the whole of life begins to make sense. Our inherent insecurities begin to dissolve. Our pain and confusions are easily embraced and healed, and then they fall away. It becomes easier for us to be forgiving and loving because we see that almost all of our pain arises out of this fundamental misunderstanding that we are a separate self. We find that we are able to meet others and ourselves with this overwhelming love, which is at the core of all beings. This direct experience is all possible because we are able to see the overwhelming radiance pouring out of every living thing. And because we are no longer seeing life through the lens of ego, we no longer believe in our limiting beliefs. It is when we discover our own radiant nature that we also discover the radiant nature of all of life. We no longer see life through the lens of cold mental egoic definitions.

It is very much like when we meet our baby for the first time; life has literally ripped us wide open. We have to surrender to the fact that we are no longer in control; we have stepped into this vast Mystery. And when the baby finally comes forward, we have no definition of them. We pick them up and hold them to our chest and feel the radiance pouring out of them. We look into their eyes and see the vast Mystery of what they are. We do not look them in the eyes and say, "I know who you are, you are going to be a really bad baby," or "You are going to grow up and be a doctor just like Mommy." We have no idea who this being truly is. So when we look into their eyes and allow ourselves to experience this newborn at the level of essence, we experience their wonder, their awe, and their inherent Beauty and Divinity. However, because our egoic nature is always trying to name, label, and contextualize the unknown, ironically, a few minutes later, we attempt to put a name on our baby, which is the silliest thing imaginable. Here we have just met this Divine wonder, and now we are going to try and name it. This is what egos continually do: name and define the indefinable. It is not that our ego is bad, it serves a practical purpose to have a name. But when we define anything, we create a sense of separation between us and it, and it and life. We begin to see the label and fill this label with our ideas, and as we do this we get further and further from the truth or direct experience of what is before us. Our tendency to label life, to put names on things is not bad or wrong, it is actually quite practical. The problem only comes when we mistake the label for the thing and fill the label with our projections and judgments. When we say, "I have a boy," we cover our child with all of our definitions of a boy. We no longer see a Mystery, and we begin to try and figure out who this person is according to our beliefs and projections about what a boy is. When we name him Charles, we create a label and try to fill this label with what we know and project upon him. We say, "He is a boy and he is 8 pounds. He has blue eyes and looks like his grandfather Charles. He will grow up and become a great businessman." The more that we fill in the mystery of who he is, *the further we get from who he truly is.*

When my first baby came into the world, I could not name her for days. All I saw was this ancient Divine Presence. The experience with my second baby has been the same; it has been several months since she was born and I still have trouble calling her by a name. Now that my first daughter is sixteen years old, she has filled in her presence with her humanity, and yet, even when she is tough with me (as some teenagers are), in my heart is a total love for her. When I see her, I experience her quiet depth, beauty, and radiance. There are times when I become carried away in my parental frustrations of raising a teenager, but because I know who she truly is, it is easy for me to come back to this unconditional love and to an understanding and experiencing of her Divinity.

With my second daughter, my wife often tells me to call our new baby by her name, but it is difficult for me. I do not see a child called "Ani." What I see is a bundle of radiance, joy, and Beauty before me (who sometimes cries and needs a new diaper). However, not many of us are willing to live in an undefined way in a world without divisions, judgments, and labels. But the way of any true spiritual path is one of freedom, found immersed in the great Mystery of life. Fortunately, this experience is not too far away from us; it is at the core of our being. Take one step out of our egoic nature and it is here. All of us live with an egoic nature that will continually try to veil Reality to one degree or another. But as we awaken, we begin to have a choice to see life either from the openness of our hearts or to habitually project our past onto our current experience. We have the choice to see and experience life in a fresh way, without concepts or expectations—we can see and experience life as *radiant and alive.*

This is why the teachings on awakening out of egoic identification are so deeply important and practical—because as we awaken, our life reorients toward pure perception, oneness, compassion, love, and unity. As we surrender to this awakening more and more, we surrender our egoic identity, our will, and allow something much greater to see and live through us. As this surrender deepens and our awakening matures, this force of Divinity begins to live through us as Us, and our life radically changes.

Practice: All is One—the Direct Experience of Oneness

Find a quiet space and contemplate these questions:

- Who am I beyond thought and emotion?

- Who am I as I sit here with no thought?

- What is actually here and present in the absence of thought and emotion, past and future?

As you ponder these questions, feel your presence. Let go into the space of what you are. Give yourself permission simply to feel your subtle energy body, especially from the neck down. Notice the presence of your heart, the rise and fall of your breath, and simply rest here.

Practice: The Radiance of Nature

1. Walk out into nature and find a quiet space to sit in meditation. Gently allow your gaze to rest upon your view. Give yourself

permission to let go of all thinking and commenting on the environment. Just be here with the rise and fall of your breath.

2. Notice how you feel when you do not think, judge, or comment upon what lies before you. Give yourself permission to merge with your environment. Notice how you feel as you let go and allow all sense of division to fall away. From this space of non-division, see and feel the quiet radiance of Life Itself.

3. Notice that all of Life is subtly radiating with light and energy, and that you too, the very space of awareness that you are, are subtly radiating with light and energy.

4. From this space ask yourself, "How am I separate from the radiance of nature?" Rest in this space.

Chapter Four

Stepping Into Our Divinity

The core of every practice.

MY TEACHER CONTINUALLY REMINDED ME that the purpose of spirituality and all spiritual teachings was to directly experience the Divine in every aspect of life. Beyond dogma, philosophy, and correct posture and asana practice, beyond knowing all the Buddhist and Hindu gods, and beyond our silly spiritual clothes and costumes, the most important teaching is to directly experience the Divine here and now. To experience this, we must first practically know how to unhook from our habitual minds and the belief in this mind as our identity—as who and what we know ourselves to be. It is only when we let go of our egoic identity that we can discover something much greater. The instructions here are very simple and *everyone* has the ability to do this; unfortunately, most of us choose instead to remain in the confusing, painful (yet entertaining) world of the mind. But if we want to be free from ego and connected deeply with our heart, we will follow this dharma wholeheartedly.

Our usual state of mind is very much like a trance state where we have no control over our thoughts and have little awareness of who is driving this thing called "me." Therefore, to free ourselves from this trance state, first and foremost we must *slow down*. We will never unhook from our minds unless we slow down the constant stream of egoic stimulation throughout our lives.

Our mind's trance state is sustained through the belief and seduction in the constant movement of our thoughts. To unhook from this trance, we have to slow down and choose to step back and observe what is here from a space of mindfulness awareness. We must be willing to observe that which is in our consciousness. We have to be willing to see that our thoughts, feelings, and sensations all come and go within the space of our being. The practice is to stop or break the habitual attachment to our thoughts, beliefs, and desires, and then simply notice the very presence in which these thoughts and feelings arise. What this practically means is that we stop and *feel* the direct experience of our very own presence.

We can all do this right here and right now. We can feel the aliveness in our heart, in our chest, in our belly, and in the space we call our mind. We can notice that this space which we are is already perfect and already free, completely alive and beautiful. If we struggle with this practice, it simply means we need to *slow down to a stop*. We need to step into silence for a few hours and break this cycle of thought and attachment. We must meditate on what we truly are, beyond our mind. If we can break this attachment for even just a few minutes, we can discover this Divine presence within us. It is when we give ourselves to this shift in identity—the shift out of our egoic nature and into the direct experience of our Being—that our lives will be forever changed.

We will come back to this practice of directly experiencing ourselves at the level of essence again and again throughout this book. If we apply this practice in a sincere manner, it will simply become our natural way of being. If we never discover how to consciously be who we are beyond mind as the love and space of our own presence, we will never know ourselves as Divine. No amount of meditation, philosophy, dogma, chanting, or asana practice can get us there. The experience of being the Divine can only come by our direct experience; anything else will be empty practices, temporal states, or just mental philosophy. To know ourselves as Divine, we must experience ourselves as Divine and then give ourselves fully to this Divinity. The good news is that *this is what we already are* in our true nature. This is what we have always been, long before the first thought passed through our minds. The consciousness of every baby that incarnates into this world is awake alive spaciousness and lives in a state of total oneness. It is through the introduction of the egoic mind, when we are toddlers, that we become entranced by our own thinking and forget this Divinity. This Divinity is not lost, but silently waiting in the background for us to again discover what we are and always have been.

Practice: Notice the Busy-ness of Your Mind

1. Put everything down and sit quietly.

2. Can you notice how quickly your mind moves throughout the day? Can you notice how busy your mind can become and how it can fabricate worlds and realities that are not happening in this present moment?

3. Notice the stream of thoughts and feelings floating through your consciousness.

4. Notice how many thoughts pull you into their story and habitual ways of acting or behaving.

5. Notice how you are attached to certain thoughts and are unwilling to let go of them.

6. Be still and know that you are the space of awareness, witnessing the entire dance of the story of desire, aversion, and attachment.

Practice: Feel and Experience Your Own Self

This practice is simple, yet requires a gentle discipline:

1. Simply feel the aliveness of your own heart. Give yourself fully to this loving presence of your heart.

2. Experience the spaciousness of your mind, the very space out of which your thoughts arise. Directly experience the Silence before your thoughts arise. Give yourself to this direct experience of luminosity, spaciousness, and silence. Feel how brilliant and alive this luminosity is. Feel how vast this spaciousness is. Feel the timeless nature of Silence. Notice that this Silence is everywhere, within and around you, despite the presence of thoughts and sounds.

3. Give yourself over to this experience again and again. If your mind comes forward and seduces you again, notice the *feeling* of the mind and gently come back to the direct experience of your own presence. Feel the Radiance of your heart fill this spacious Silence that you are.

4. Directly experience your own Divinity while you practice your yoga, meditation, chanting, prayer work, or whatever you may find yourself doing. This is your constant invitation.

If we love and respect ourselves in the deepest way, we will make the evolution of our humanity our highest priority. Our path is the most important movement in our lives. If we are going to consciously walk this path, we must cultivate a commitment to our truth and the perseverance to never give up the journey. If we choose to live in this way, our lives will be focused on the discovery of our innate Beauty and upon the manifestation and evolution of this Beauty in the world.

Contemplate these questions:

- Am I dedicated to this path?

- What is in the way of my dedication?

- Where do I find myself confused and walking in circles on the path?

- How do I give my power away to things that do not serve me?

- Am I willing to recommit myself to this path in a deeper and fuller way?

At first glance, this commitment may look like a selfish or narcissistic endeavor and we may ask ourselves, "Is it selfish to make discovering my own divinity a priority?" As we deeply contemplate this question, we will find that Love is the movement of God. How could knowing, experiencing, and expressing Love in our lives ever be selfish?

When we discover our divinity, it naturally spreads to those around us. It moves through us as we look into the eyes of our baby, as we speak to our friends and families, and as we move through life. An amazing experience unfolds as we take the time to realize our Divinity; we begin to discover it in everyone and everything. We will even begin to find the Divine in the things that scare us, the things that we avoid, and in the things that we wish did not exist. Contemplate these questions and see what greater truths come forward.

To truly discover that all of life is Divine, we must make the commitment to practice every day and allow ourselves to make no excuses otherwise. This means that when our minds create the ten thousand reasons why not to practice, we simply have to gently say "no" and go sit on our meditation cushion or yoga mat, or begin our prayer work—whatever our practice may be. We must commit to doing it *every day*. If we do not, we will be spun in an endless journey of our mind which will ultimately lead us from one transient thing to the next. We all know the experience of surfing the internet and going unconscious; we start surfing with one intention and then minutes or hours later find ourselves lost somewhere else. If we are going to commit ourselves to this humble discovery, it will require a great discipline within ourselves. Our time and attention are the greatest superpowers that we have. If we are not in charge of our time and attention, we become powerless on the path. When we choose to practice in a disciplined way, we focus our time and attention on our highest intention and do not allow the unconscious forces of habit, desire, addiction, and distraction to lead us in life.

Ask yourself, "Am I willing to practice every day? Am I willing to surrender my time and schedule to this great path of Awakening?"

Many individuals have come and told me how they have no time to practice. The answer I give them is quite simple: we can all get up earlier or stay up later, and we can all practice during the midst of life. I have literally not missed a day of practice in over twenty years. During this time, I have worked my way through college and graduate school, raised three children, volunteered tens of thousands of hours for my teacher and dharma centers, been married, divorced, married again, and run two businesses. I laugh when individuals tell me they do not have time to practice. We all have the same amount of time. The question is, can we align our energy with our commitment? If we want to get anywhere in life or on the spiritual path, we have to give ourselves fully to our highest intention. At a minimum, I would prescribe an hour a day of some type of formal practice, whether it is silent meditation, prayer, yoga, Bible study, chanting, or whatever it is that deeply resonates with our heart. We can start with five, ten, fifteen, or twenty minutes each day, and then work our way up to an hour, until finally our practice no longer is a practice, but simply a way of life.

If we are to be successful, we have to begin with an *unwavering commitment*. We have to say no to the things in our lives that are unnecessary. We must say no to the TV, no to mindlessly surfing the internet, no to all the ways that we unconsciously waste time. We have to say no to our endless "to do" lists and make our quest for Truth the most important thing in our lives. Even if we have jobs, careers, relationships, and children, we can still make peace, love, and freedom our number one priority. There is no greater need in this world than peace and love. We do not have to run away and become a monk or a nun—although some retreat time is almost always necessary to help us to solidify in this greater vision. In the midst of our busy lives, we can, however, pick up our crying baby *with peace and compassion*. We can work with our emotions with love and clarity. We can actively choose to renounce our own habitual and neurotic thoughts as they arise. We can do all these things whether we are sitting on our special Buddhist meditation cushion or waiting in line at the supermarket with two anxious children. In the midst of our busy lives, it is necessary to spend some time each day in silence. Whether we get up an hour early or wait until after we have put our children to sleep, it is greatly important to have some time each day for that which is beyond the busy egoic dance that we call our lives.

This commitment and discipline may start with us implementing our willpower. We may have to say no to an array of voices within our minds and commit by sheer will to sit for an hour or to practice our asana sequence each day. We may rely on our will for years or even decades to keep us on the straight and narrow path. But in the end, our practice must arise from and be fueled by the sincerity of our hearts, or it will become just another egoic endeavor. I am always surprised at how many people practice for egoic reasons, whether it is to have a perfect yoga body or for some perceived status within a sangha or church; sometimes our practice is even just a strategy for escaping life. But if we want to know the truth of our nature, our intentions must be clear and free of ego. Our egoic intentions and our willpower can greatly lead us astray if we are not careful. It is wise to always check that the heart is leading the way on the spiritual path.

Our willpower is a great strength to possess at the beginning of the path. It makes certain we show up to practice each day. But if we do not know how to eventually surrender our personal will, we will find ourselves practicing for egoic reasons, such as pride, because we are stuck in a habitual way of being. Over the years, I have met many grumpy meditators who could benefit from doing less meditation and more yoga, and others who could learn to laugh and be more compassionate with their children. Our will is very much like a double-edged sword; it can be absolutely essential to rely on the strength of our will in the beginning on the path, and yet, after we are established in practice as a part of our everyday lives and have realized the gift of our practice, our will must give way to our heart. If not, we may find ourselves suffering from pride, overzealousness, or inflexibility.

I recommend a *gentle discipline*. A strong will can be helpful if we are beginning a new practice or habit or if we have a "monkey mind" and emotions that run us all over the place, creating ten thousand reasons why not to practice. Our willpower can help us to see that we have a choice in how we relate to our minds. Through our discipline, we discover that we actually have a choice whether or not to listen to our very own thoughts, as convincing as they might seem. Through stepping out of our minds, we see that in every moment we have the choice to be free or to be unconscious. In this freedom lies our power— our choice to practice and live in alignment with our hearts. This is a choice we must make a thousand times in a day, until at some point this Love, this Intelligence that we glimpse when we practice, simply takes over our lives.

Our commitment to practice is our first step, and after some time we become established in this practice. Then our practice evolves to fully honoring the arising wisdom of our heart through staying vigilant in our intention to know God in every aspect of our lives. However, there is a danger at this point in the path; we can once again become prideful or arrogant due to our new realizations. Many individuals who experience spiritual states of consciousness, profound spiritual awakenings, or come to some perceived "end point" of the spiritual path give up their practices and choose to live as the Divine Presence which they have discovered themselves to be. But we must remind ourselves that even the Buddha continued to practice, although he was fully realized. A long list of yogis, priests, saints, and sages have had a profound spiritual realization and then later have become arrogant, power hungry, or seduced by desire because they were not humble enough to continue to practice—to continue to surrender their humanity.

Over time, what we discover is that our practice will grow, change, and become more heart centered and gentle. After many years of deep commitment to the path of Truth, this practice will become a way of being and not so much a discipline or practice. But it is always wise to carry with us the attitude of compassionate mindfulness. It is said that although Buddha faced "Mara"—the manifestations of fear, aggression, and desire—on the night before his enlightenment, he also faced these forces throughout the rest of his life. Because he carried with him a gentle discipline, he was able to meet Mara throughout his life with compassionate mindfulness, and thus not be seduced by Mara. It would be wise for us to do the same.

Spiritual practice keeps us honest and in check. If we are not careful, at any point along the path we can again become seduced by our unconsciousness; therefore, it is wise to practice wholeheartedly until our last breath in this realm.

Practice: Commitment and Perseverance as a Way of Life

- Try out a variety of spiritual practices such as various forms of yoga, meditation, chanting, dharma study, dance, contemplative prayer, and simply sitting in silence. After testing an array of practices, commit yourself to the practice which resonates the most with your heart.

- Start your practice for twenty minutes each day and then work up to one hour or longer daily. Notice how you feel inwardly as you commit to your practice. Notice which distractions call you away from your practice. Commit your life to alignment with your spiritual practices and opening to the truth of your heart.

- Each week schedule an additional hour or more beyond your normal practice, where you give yourself permission to simply *rest as awareness*. Sit in silence and watch the movements of your mind. Watch the coming and going of thoughts, watch the trees blow in the wind, or the clouds float through the sky. Give yourself permission to not think, but to simply feel what is arising within yourself. After sitting for some time, get up and walk in silence. Feel, be, and experience life just as it is... open, spacious, and free. Notice how differently you feel when you practice in this informal yet openhearted way.

- After practicing every day for a month or more, sit down and reflect upon how you feel differently after committing to practicing each day. Is there more space in your mind and body? How do you feel energetically? Where do you struggle with practice? What could you be doing more or less of? Do you feel more peace, love, compassion, or spaciousness?

Practice is a way of life.

To begin to get in touch with the innate Divinity of our own heart space, it is important to develop a sincere spiritual practice. If our spiritual practices are going to help us to grow, change, transform, and actually embody our Divinity, these practices must become a way of life. If we sit down in the morning and practice meditation for ten minutes, we are essentially taking a break from our ego. But to truly wake up out of ego and into our true nature, we have to be willing to embody a radically new way of living and being in the world in each and every moment.

If we are just now consciously stepping on the path, a ten-minute meditation may be a step forward for us. But if we want to live in a totally new way, we must be willing to take a leap in consciousness. To leap fully with all of our self, we must be deeply honest and choose to be all in. Our practice will only become a way of being and have the power to transform and free us if we are fully willing to jump in the ocean of Divinity. Too many of us on the spiritual path have the attitude that we are just going to dip our toe in the water, and then we wonder why nothing changes. If we want to experience a radical shift in our state of consciousness, we have to jump fully into the ocean of Life. What this means, practically, is that we meet our lives in every moment from the beauty and wisdom of our hearts. For most of us, this is foreign territory.

In order to begin our practice, we must first cultivate the attitude that "I am going to give this 100%." This is very important, because if we are not 100% in our intention and in our willingness, then we will be at the mercy of the movement of our habitual minds.

Once, during Satsang (a spiritual meeting), I was leading a group in meditation. After our meditation, I asked one of the individuals to describe the essence of his experience. I invited him to go inward and to see and experience the depth of who and what he was beyond his egoic nature. He replied, "I don't want to right now." If we are not willing to be open to investigating our experience, then we will continue to stay stuck in our ego.

I asked this same question of someone else at the meeting who was willing to be open to and investigate her experience. Very quickly tears began to roll down her cheeks as she shared that, with this invitation, she had been able to experience her Divinity for the first time in her life. She went on to share that she was able to release a deeply held sadness from her heart. All of this took place because she was willing to open beyond the walls of her habitual mind and way of being. Through her willingness, the energy of the room became filled with a humility and innocence, and everyone present sincerely benefited from her courage and willingness.

This attitude of being fully open and willing is what is required if we want to truly know ourselves as Divine. There is no other way.

Chapter Five

The Necessity of Slowing Down

THE ATTITUDES OF WILLINGNESS, OPENNESS, AND GIVING all of oneself are completely necessary if we want to awaken to our true nature. Without these attitudes, the only way we will grow is if we are forced to, which is what Life will actually do if we do not cooperate with Her intelligence and movement. It is through sincere practice that we can learn to open to this Intelligence. All true spiritual practices bring us into alignment with the Truth, Intelligence, and Grace of God.

One of the most powerful practices we can adopt is slowing down. The act of slowing down breaks our entrancement with our egoic nature. It creates a sense of space between what we are and the movement of our minds. There are so many ways that we can slow down in our lives. We can take deep breaths for a few minutes each hour at work and on our drive home. We can look up at the vastness of the sky and give ourselves permission to merge into the hugeness and emptiness that is always here. We can walk slowly on our lunch break and commune with the flowers and the grass. Or perhaps, if we are deeply dedicated, we could sit for a few hours a day in silent meditation. The simple truth is that the more we slow down, the easier it will be to see clearly and to step into the Peace and spaciousness that is here in every moment.

Slowing down is the primary practice of meditation. But seated meditation is not the only way to step into this space and peace. We can practice yoga, we can go for a walk, and we can turn our phones and electronic devices off and simply see and hear the spacious silence all around us. We can make a date with the sunset or sunrise, we can hike or camp, we can choose to not speak unnecessarily and have a day or week of silence in nature. We can simply slow down at work and yet continue working with mindfulness. We can slow down with our children and yet continue parenting mindfully. The opportunities are countless in which we can choose to slow down with our children, relationships, friends, and families, and not rush them or ourselves. When we choose to do so, everyone is much happier, present, and at ease.

When we slow down, our ego begins to lose its momentum. In fact, the quicker, busier, and more dramatic we are, the more we will experience our ego. Slowing down is the fastest and most effective way to experience inner clarity and sanity. What slowing down requires is that we let go of our allegiance to our thoughts and beliefs and step into the present moment. When we deeply examine this force of ego within us, we discover how attached we are to our thoughts, agendas, philosophies, and religious and political beliefs.

Our ego is not made up of only thoughts and feelings. Our egoic nature is driven by psychological forces, one of which is the projected illusion that we have control over our lives. While in theory this is helpful and keeps us alive, it is a projected myth, for none of us truly has control over our lives. Life will do what Life is going to do, despite our attempts to outsmart Life. But our egoic nature still tries, through projecting a perceived sense of control over our lives. Most of us do not recognize this projected sense of control until we are in a real-life situation where we are shown that we do not have control, in this moment or any.

Despite momentary realizations that we are not in control of our lives, our ego continually falsely assumes that we are. All of us have within us a micromanaging force which tries hard to control ourselves, the environment, and the people around us. Yet Reality shows us that Life will do whatever it does, whether we are there to micromanage it or not. The practice for those of us on the path is to trust that life is not going to fall apart if we unhook from all the unconscious controlling ways that we meet life. This can be a huge step for most of us; we arrogantly assume that if we are not there to micromanage life, that life will stop and everything will fall apart. When we wake up to this wisdom, we discover that the opposite happens. If we slow ourselves to a stop, we begin to experience Peace, and Life begins to take care of the rest. Life reminds us of this basic truth when we are sick and home in bed or when we go on a spiritual retreat or a vacation. Life goes on, the world continues to function without our micromanagement of it. The world does not need to be controlled. When we open to this basic truth, the controlling nature of ego is liberated.

This is our ongoing invitation, to unhook from the trance of our egoic nature (and the perceived sense of control that goes with it) and give ourselves the gift of slowing down. When we give ourselves the gift of completely slowing down to a stop, we will discover something extraordinary. Our direct experience will be of oneness, because when our mind stops completely, we directly experience non-division, unity, and peace. But as soon as we begin to get involved with our controlling or micromanaging thoughts once again, we will find ourselves back in the world of separation. We will again imagine a separation between us and the beautiful Reality that is always here.

Practice: Slow Down—Breathe, Feel, Experience

1. Stop, right now. Stop. Put everything down.

2. Feel into your body; experientially feel the thoughts, emotions, and sensations in your body right now.

3. Ask yourself, "Where am I tight or tense within my body and nervous system?" Anywhere that you feel tightness, tension, irritability, agitation, criticism, judgments, fear, anxiety, intense emotions, subtle emotions, or subtle holding provides you with physical clues that point to the places where you rush, resist, control, and are fighting with life.

4. Drop in here. Open to these feelings and breathe into them. Be with these feelings as long as it takes to feel a sense of peace here.

5. Repeat this practice throughout your day as often as you can.

Practice: Basic Meditation

Without a daily meditation practice of some kind, it is hard to progress in a meaningful and profound way on the spiritual path. Find, adopt, and seek training in a meditation practice which resonates with your heart.

If you are new to meditation, explore various schools of meditation and find one which works. There are many different types of meditations offered in this book which you may find helpful.

The basic meditation teaching is as follows:

1. Sit comfortably and still, with your spine straight and your hands resting in your lap or on your thighs with your palms facing up.

2. Bring your attention inward and breathe, feel, and experience while not engaging with any passing thought.

3. Be here now.

4. Feel, experience, and open.

If you are challenged with staying seated for very long during meditation, begin with shorter meditation sessions (e.g., five, ten, or fifteen minutes) and sit a little longer each day.

If you are struggling when you meditate, please remember that it is important to commit to your meditation times (sit for the entire period you decided on) and recognize that it is only the mind that is causing the struggle.

You can hold this mind with great love and gentleness and let it know that *everything will be okay*—that you can just sit quietly together for this period of time.

Open, open, open to the beauty and innocence of your heart. Rest here in the space of meditation.

Chapter Six

Meditation

The courage to face ourselves.

A DAILY MEDITATION PRACTICE IS ESSENTIAL for anyone who is interested in waking up to a greater reality beyond the egoic self. It is a rare soul who actually awakens without at some point practicing some form of meditation in a committed and disciplined way. The practice of meditation orients us toward silence and opens us to deeply experience what we are.

When I teach or guide meditation, there are a few main instructions I offer. The first is to be willing to let go of our allegiance to our minds. That means we must be willing to step out of our mind and simply *allow everything to be as it is*. This in no way means that we must stop or control or resist our mind. We are simply choosing to step out of our mental thought stream and refusing to go along with it on its never-ending journey—for we are not our thoughts, but that which witnesses our thoughts. When we sit down together to practice meditation, I invite students to experience what it feels like in the mind and to notice the feeling of thinking. Next, I instruct them to unhook from thinking as their center of identification and allow their sense of awareness to fall backwards into the spacious presence out of which all thoughts arise. As we step out of our limited mental view, we open into the entire feeling nature of our being and bring awareness to every part of it. Practically speaking, we bring our attention to the feeling nature of our heart, our back, our belly, our pelvis, our arms, and our legs. We feel into every part of our being.

We can do this all at once if we are naturally open, or we can go one by one through our body parts, opening the various centers and areas of our being until we can feel and experience this spaciousness throughout our being. We can ask, "Do I sense this spaciousness in the space of my mind, my heart, and my belly?" After you begin to notice this space within yourself, can you begin to notice this same spaciousness all around your body? Is this spaciousness within any different from the spaciousness of your room or the sky?

Yoga training is incredibly helpful for this type of meditation. The gift that yoga has brought us is a greater awareness of our subtle bodies. Our job is to step out of the mind and into this subtle realm of being, and then to simply rest here. If we get lost in thought at any point along the way, we again come back to feeling our subtle body and continue opening to our entire being. We especially open everywhere beyond our habitual mental world. And soon, what we begin to discover is that what we *are* is not limited to a thinking mind and physical body. What we are is quite huge and vast. Through sitting and meditating in this way, many of us may glimpse our true nature, but do not fully land or stabilize in our experience here. And so, most of us have work to do to clear the way for this greater realization to live through us, as Us.

Practice: Meeting Pain and Tension With Loving Kindness

When most of us begin to journey inward we may begin to experience boundlessness, and yet we may also notice where we are quite limited. As we journey inward, we will notice various places which are tight and tense and are in need of healing.

For this healing meditation, the instruction is simple:

1. Bring your awareness into any pain or tension felt in your body and breathe into it.

2. Be with it fully without wanting it to be different than it is.

3. Acknowledge whatever feeling is here, and fully breathe a sense of *okay-ness* into it.

4. Continue this breathing until you feel a release, a greater softening or healing of the pain or tension.

This practice requires that we be more courageous than our biological wiring, whose function is to seek pleasure and avoid pain. When we choose to practice, we are taking the time and space to presently acknowledge and respond with love to the tension, pain, or wounds within us from the openness of our Divinity. We are not doing this as a mental activity to change or get rid of pain. We are embracing what is within us as an act of love from our own heart space. As we meet ourselves in this way, the pain and tension are invited to relax, release, and heal in the spacious radiance that we are.

It takes courage to do this work. The primary reason most of us do not meditate is because we are afraid of all the painful, hidden, and rejected places that live within us. It is easier to avoid our inner world than to embrace it. Many beginning meditators struggle with sitting silently because, more often than not, this silence is filled with the arising of repressed emotional energies. For some individuals, this practice of silently witnessing and loving old pain and heartache is too much and they give up their practice soon after they have begun. But before one chooses to give up, it is important to understand why this pain from the past is arising and disturbing our silent practice.

When we begin to practice with an open heart, repressed emotional energies come forward within our consciousness wanting our love and attention. These energies come forward wanting to be healed by our loving presence and released into the spaciousness of our true nature. Our work is to courageously open to both the vastness and Divinity of what we are, as well as to our humanity. As we do so, we discover freedom and compassion. We open to our true nature and begin to transform our humanity so that one day this humanity can begin to fully reflect the goodness, love, and truth of our Divinity in our everyday lives.

This work will be as powerful as our courage and commitment to it. If we simply practice meditation once and buy some prayer beads, not much is going to change within us. Yet, if we practice as if our life depended upon it, our life would radically transform. But transformation comes with a price. It requires that we sacrifice our old habitual and guarded life for a greater life. It is through this sacrifice that we will experience great change within us.

If we meet each repressed emotion that arises from a space of love and compassion, it will heal and release, and we will begin to feel more space and love within us. In truth, this loving presence is already here within us. Meditation is a time for us to reconnect with what we essentially are. But it is also a time for us to see that we have pain and suffering covering our innate goodness. If our practice is not both about awakening *and healing*, then our brightness will never truly have a chance to shine. Our commitment to practice is a commitment to fully healing, loving, and honoring what we fully are.

Chapter Seven

Turning Awareness Upon Itself

IF WE WANT TO WAKE UP TO OUR TRUE NATURE, WE MUST become aware of the one who simply sees—the one who is awake and aware of Buddha nature. To awaken to this space of our true nature, we must drop all attachment to thought, emotions, and body. We must see that "I am *not* these thoughts or emotions. I am that which *witnesses thoughts and emotions*." From here we take a step further. We *turn seeing upon itself*. We turn awareness upon itself. We do this by directly experiencing the one who sees. You can do this right now; you can stop and directly experience the one who is seeing these words on the page. Notice what happens when you do this... your mind activity stops, and you discover who you are before thought arises. You may notice a gentle stillness, an openness and innocence—all right here, right now. This is our essence. This is our true nature. This is what we actually are in every moment but have forgotten because we have been in the trance state of our mind for so long.

If we notice that thoughts arise while meditating, we pay no attention to them. Instead we turn around and *notice the one that notices*. We turn our awareness upon itself. For most of us, this space will be quite confusing because habitually, our practical everyday awareness only looks outward. We look to see who's around us, if there are any threats or things we want in our environment, or if there is any work that needs to be done. We look to see if there are any problems to deal with or if our hair and clothes look just right for yoga class.

During meditation, instead of looking outward, we turn our awareness upon itself. We allow ourselves to notice and *become* the purity, the spaciousness, and the vibrancy of the one who sees, and we acknowledge that in truth, *we are none other than this.* We discover that thoughts, emotions, sensations, and even movements of Grace arise and fall within this silent vibrant awareness that is always already here. We see that our thoughts and thinking are simply a trance state. What we are is *that which is silently here in every moment*—our presence. We rest as this presence and are invited to rest here forever. In this space, we continue directly experiencing life from this openhearted vast perspective. Whether we are driving to work or practicing yoga, we live as this presence. This is our constant invitation.

As we embody our True Nature more and more, we become confident in our inherent freedom and Divinity. As we do so, what we discover is that life truly is Divine.

Practice: Turning Awareness Upon Itself

1. Find a quiet space and notice the thoughts floating through your consciousness. Notice that there are thoughts and the one who sees the thoughts. There are emotions and the one who feels the emotions. There is a body and the one who sees and feels the body and its sensations. Who is it that notices the thoughts, emotions, sensations, and body? Who or what is here that is beyond the movement of thought, emotions, and sensations? Who is it that is here and inhabits this body? Rest and experience what you are beyond the movements of mind.

2. While sitting quietly, contemplate these questions:

   ▪ Who am I when no thought is present?

- Who is it that observes thoughts? What does this presence that I am, feel like?

- Can I feel and experience the spaciousness and silence of my own nature?

- What is here that is already perfectly quiet and universally good?

3. Allow awareness to notice the thoughts, emotions, and sensations floating through your consciousness. Now, stop looking outward and allow awareness to turn inward and look directly at your own self. Rest here, in this space of silence and luminosity.

4. If you find yourself lost in thought again, simply turn awareness upon itself again. Become aware of awareness and rest here. Smile and let go into the beauty and silence of your true nature.

5. When you have completed your formal meditation practice of turning awareness upon itself and you are walking forward throughout your day, keep these questions in mind:

- Can I notice the quiet presence of awareness, right here, right now?

- Can I notice that there is a quiet presence continually witnessing every moment of my everyday life?

- Can I notice that this awareness requires no effort, no doing?

- Do I realize that I am awake awareness already, right here and right now?

~ Chapter Eight ~

Opening to a Greater Divinity

THROUGHOUT HISTORY THERE HAVE BEEN COUNTLESS scandals among leaders or followers of organized religion. For many, this has greatly tarnished the place of God in spirituality and our lives. Unfortunately, for those of us who have been on the receiving end of this pain or trauma, there is often an ending of one's relationship with God because of how a religious figure or organization treated us. While it is understandable to leave a church if one experienced abuse there, we must acknowledge that the abuse came from the shadow side of a human being, not from God Herself. I can painfully remember that within my childhood church there were many scandals and victims of abuse, and I fully acknowledge the horror of such violence and trauma. It is through discernment though that we know that this pain and abuse are rooted in the confusion of man, and that these individuals are not God's true representatives. I can remember that, as a young adult, I never quite paid attention to the church priests; instead, I chose to open my heart to the direct experience of God and see for myself what God was and is. The more I opened to this direct experience, the more I have lived in awe of Her Grace.

This next chapter is an invitation to join me in this direct experience of Grace. But again, I would like to reiterate that when I speak of God, I am referring to the God of Love, of Light, of Peace, and of Compassion. Not the god of the church which allows or tolerates abuse, not the Sunday-school version of god, or the god of one judgmental and exclusive religious tradition. Many of our ancient religious traditions, with their countless scandals and desire to control or maintain followers, do not accurately represent the True God of Love and Compassion, but rather represent an archaic God who is angry or judgmental or only loves the "chosen people." Let us together let go of old and outdated views of God and examine *experientially* the True God of Love and see for ourselves what God actually is, beyond ideas, dogmas, or religious traditions.

In addition to the previous instructions of opening to our True Nature and healing our humanity, another practice that is core to these teachings is being receptive to the Direct Experience of God. In order to begin to orient one's heart to this type of practice, we must be humble and desire to know God in our Hearts. To practice in this way, we first must cultivate a prayer-like attitude of humbly opening to that which is *Greater* than ourselves. Most meditation practices begin by opening to awareness and letting everything be as it is. We are actively choosing to not get involved with our busy thinking minds. We let go, and open into the spaciousness of awareness throughout our being. It is from this space of openness and receptivity that we bring our awareness to our crown chakra on the top of our head and to our heart chakra, and cultivate a prayer-like attitude of willingness and humility to receive Grace from the Divine.

This Grace may come in the experience of a feeling or sensations arising within us; perhaps a warm movement of energy descending from above or coming up from below. Or it may feel like radiance in our heart, third eye, or belly. It may come in the form of light, radiant peace, spaciousness, or a healing energy. There are countless ways in which we can receive Grace from the vast compassion of the Universe. We are simply opening to this Grace and Intelligence and allowing it to have *Her way with us*.

Many individuals, especially from the Buddhist and nondual traditions, are unfamiliar with experiencing the Divine and the direct transmission of Grace because they focus solely on the experience of awareness or on emptiness. But why limit oneself from experiencing the vast and intuitive Intelligence of the Universe? Why not be open and learn from the very force that created all? This practice that I am offering requires one to Trust that God knows better than we do. It requires that we be humble, open, and receptive to a transmission of Grace and healing energies specifically tailored for us, by the Mother of the Universe.

The first and most important instruction that my teacher gave me was that *the spiritual path is primarily about the direct experience of God—in you and as You.* For two decades, this work with my teacher deepened to the experience of living in Grace, not just during meditation but throughout my life. And an understanding that if I am not feeling flooded with Grace in every moment of my life, it means I am somehow out of alignment with Reality. When this is recognized, it becomes quite clear that realignment with the Truth is the way back home to a life of Grace. Most individuals cherish these rare moments of Grace. But instead of cherishing a rare moment, this invitation is to invite God to awaken *in you and as You in all moments.*

After meeting with and teaching thousands of individuals, I have discovered that most spiritual people are quite unfamiliar with the direct experience of Divinity and have little to no direct relationship with God. They may have ideas or philosophies about God, and sometimes great pain or trauma around their experience of organized religions, but no direct or lasting relationship *with God.* We can start to bridge this gap by way of prayer—a humble and openhearted receptivity toward God. Our prayer must not be about empty words, but rather about experientially opening our seven chakra centers and the fullness of our being to the direct experience of Grace. We do this by opening ourselves to this greater force—by including the Divine in our lives in an intimate way. Through this ongoing prayer of "Lord come into me, in every aspect of my being," this experience of Divinity can become a lifelong experiential relationship. This relationship can become so deep and united that one day we no longer can tell the difference between our humanity and our Divinity. What it requires is our humility and a willingness to open and to receive and align with the energies of the Divine in our life.

Many of us already experience these flows of energy without being fully conscious of them. We may walk into a church or yoga studio or dharma center and feel a warm and loving presence. We may notice the *light and innocence* pouring out of a newborn baby. We may experience a great Peace and spaciousness when we stand on a cliff overlooking the ocean. To become more open to this Grace in our lives, we are invited to sit down, open our heart, and simply pray and offer ourselves to God by saying, "I am open to receiving your Grace."

Unfortunately, in many modern spiritual circles, a great number of individuals have denied a God outside of themselves, while at the same time giving their egoic minds full permission to operate in the name of some form of "spiritual autonomy." Many individuals cite that Buddha ignored the notion of God, but this is not true. Buddha spent years as a yogi, practicing many forms of meditation, mantra, and worship practices, and he eventually realized the truth of his being as vast spacious awareness. He did not teach about the experience of God because he wanted his teachings to be simple and concise and focused solely on awakening to the direct experience of Awareness. In the modern spiritual world, there are far too many individuals who follow the Buddha's path in an exclusive and even closed-minded way. We must remember, the Buddha was not closed-minded; he was trained in many forms of meditation and practiced for years before coming to his own teaching. Unfortunately, many Buddhists practice within the shadow of a strict exclusive idealism and miss out on the profound experience of Grace. For most individuals, this strict exclusive idealism is rooted in a false or egoic autonomy; not the type of autonomy that comes from the discovery of our inherent wholeness. This false egoic autonomy is a form of egoic confidence which arises out of arrogance and insecurity. Our True Nature arises out of humility and an open heart. If we are going to be open to receiving a greater Divinity than ourselves, we must be humble enough to allow God's grace to flow into our being and our lives.

Choosing to open to a Graced-filled path may possibly be the most amazing gift we ever give ourselves. Our life soon will be filled with so many mystical and healing energies that our experience will become unimaginably wonderful. To open to this Grace, we must make some time each day to sit quietly. As we sit reverently, we open to the movement of the Divine in our lives.

We may begin this practice while in formal meditation or any time we are quiet. We allow this Grace to enter us and to spread out to every aspect of our lives, no matter if we are sitting on a meditation cushion or shopping for a new car. Why should any aspect of our life not include a Divinity that wants nothing else but to shower us with Grace?

Practice: Opening to the Direct Experience of God

1. Find yourself a comfortable seat. Become quiet and open your heart to God.

2. Invite Her presence into you. Call upon God, "Lord come into me and fill me with your Grace, your Peace and wonder. I open

to you now and forever. Make yourself at home in my humanity."

3. With this prayer-like attitude, gently notice the presence of God coming into you. Bring your attention to your crown and heart chakras and simply be open and receptive to God's Grace. Be patient, open, and willing to receive.

Practice: Investigating My Relationship with the Divine

Contemplate these questions deeply:

- What is my relationship with God? Do I know God? Or do I simply have thoughts about God and no real relationship directly with God? Do I have an old, archaic understanding or way of relating to God? Do I fear God or do I trust in God? Is my heart open to the direct experience of God?

- Do I know that this world is good or do I fear this world? Do I blame God for my pain and suffering? Can I acknowledge that this world is a world of growth and evolution?

- Do I have trauma or negative beliefs about God because of my experience with dogmatic religious environments or people? Has organized religion left me upset and angry at God? Is this anger God's fault or the religion's fault? Am I willing to be open again to the direct experience of God, despite having experienced pain or trauma from religious people or environments?

- Do I sincerely want to know the God of Love, Compassion, and Peace? Am I willing to lay down my old painful beliefs about God and open to a greater experience of Love?

Chapter Nine

Yoga

PRACTICING YOGA HAS THE POWER TO AWAKEN US to our "Beingness" more quickly than most other spiritual practices, because yoga gets us out of our heads and into our bodies within moments of practicing. The instructions given in most yoga classes are the same: breathe, relax, and feel what is within you. Let go of the day, let go of your thoughts, and simply be here now. It is these gentle instructions which are so healing for all of us. The most basic instructions are the most powerful and transformative. Without understanding how to let go and simply be, we will never progress on the path.

Too often, we approach our spiritual life from the perspective of our minds. At some point we must be humble enough to lose faith in the arrogance of our minds and realize that spiritual awakening is a *being experience,* not a mental one. When I say "Beingness" I am referring to the felt energetic experience of Being. Most of us live almost our entire lives lost in our minds. Yoga is an effective and powerful practice which pulls us out of our minds and grounds us into our Beingness. Through the practice of yoga, we begin to awaken our subtle energetic body, which is the space of embodied awareness and aliveness. Our subtle body is the space of our chakras, subtle energetic nervous system, and our connection to the spiritual realms. Through years of deeply practicing yoga in this intimate way, we begin to embody our subtle energetic body more fully and beingness becomes our way of life.

When we come to our yoga mats, we are called to bring our awareness out of the trance of our minds and to our bodies. However, many people avoid being in their body because their body is full of aches and pains, anxiety or depression, and uncomfortable feelings. Our bodies are *feeling instruments* and our outer world often does not feel good or safe. Most of us have had difficult, painful lives and have repressed and stored this pain in the body. But if we want to live in a way which is fearlessly free, we have to be willing to fully feel what is within us. Our bodies are designed to feel on multiple levels, but they are not designed to be storage facilities for pain for long periods of time. If we store this pain rather than release it from our bodies, they will become sick or filled with disease. In order to release this pain from our bodies, we must be willing to first become lovingly present with what is within us, which begins the process of naturally releasing pain from our being.

We have the ability to feel and become present on four primary levels: the physical level, the mental level, the emotional level, and the intuitive or subtle energetic level—the level of our chakras. When we experience painful or negative feelings within any of these levels, what most of us habitually do is attempt to ignore and avoid these feelings. Many of us try to escape to our minds or to some transcendent space, because it is here where we feel the least. For example, if we experience emotional pain, most of us retreat into our minds and create a story about how this pain should not be here and how this pain or experience should not have happened to us. We tend to hide in our minds behind a wall of arguments and judgments, never really giving ourselves permission to feel this emotional pain and the accompanying natural process of letting it go. As we distance ourselves from our pain, we actually prolong it. Instead of feeling the intensity of the emotion as it arises and allowing it to dissipate, we repress it and escape to our minds, prolonging both our experience of it and our letting go of it. If we become caught up in a story about the pain in our mind, the pain is then experienced less intensely in a felt sense way because we have distanced ourselves from the actual pain experienced in the body.

Pain, when fully felt and experienced, naturally releases quickly.

Upon reflection, most of us discover that much of our life is simply a reaction to an unwillingness to feel what is within us. Yoga is the invitation to fearlessly embody ourselves and to be fully present to what is here, even if it is unpleasant.

Practice: Measure My Beingness

A good test to measure if you are living in your Being nature is to ask yourself these questions:

- How much do I feel right now?

- Am I able to feel in every part of my being?

- Am I hiding and avoiding pain?

- In which parts of myself does my consciousness inhabit right now?

- Am I fully open throughout the totality of my physical body and my energetic body?

If we are not embodying ourselves fully, there is a good chance we are simply living in our minds. We may use the practice of yoga to begin to examine where we are not fully embodied. We can scan our bodies and notice where we are fully present. We can notice where we are able to feel and where we are not able to feel. We can begin to notice how present we can be in our heart, shoulders, belly, and hips. If we are not present in all of our being, it is usually because unconsciously we have fled or abandoned our bodies. We do this because, at some point in our lives, we have experienced some level of trauma or an overwhelming emotion, pain, or experience. This could have been the process of birth, or when our father frightened us as a child, or when we were left alone as a toddler, or any number of painful experiences. We can use our yoga practice to investigate these pains, open to them, acknowledge them, feel them, and love them, which will begin the healing and embodying process.

This is the same type of work that I do with individuals in therapy. During this process, we are invited to again feel the places within us that we have been avoiding. Perhaps we avoid these places because we were overwhelmed once by a feeling or experience and then shut down. We avoided and ultimately abandoned this part of ourselves. Through the process of therapy, yoga, or meditation we are again invited to feel that which is within us. From this place of mindfulness, we see that what is within us has passed and cannot really hurt us any longer. We may be frightened of these feelings, but as we lovingly open to them in the present moment with our feet firmly planted on the ground and allow this energy to release, we discover that it is okay to feel. We see that feelings are simply feelings and that what we are is greater than any feeling within us. We begin to realize that we do not have to fear feelings. We come to see that we do not need to run or hide. We simply need to feel what is here and allow it to go. Only then we can truly rest in every aspect of ourselves.

The practice of yoga very gracefully allows the space for this process to unfold within us. When we step on our mats, we are invited to bring our awareness to every part of our being. We open in our heart, our belly, our arms, and shoulders, and as we do, these places wake up within. As we bring our attention to our heart, we feel the emotional pain surrounding our heart and we include this in our practice; we breathe space into our heart, we love and accept any feelings or pain within us. We feel the tension and stress in our bodies, and we invite it to release. We open to the pain we have in our neck, and gently let go there. As we go through the practice, we discover that we are *feeling beings* again, not simply mental beings. As we move and stretch our bodies, we wake up our feeling nature on many different levels. Many of us do yoga and feel open, relaxed, and peaceful at the end of our practice, but are not even aware of why we feel so good. We feel good because we have taken the time to let go of the past and to awaken to our being nature, which naturally feels blissful and peaceful.

While on our yoga mat, we may notice ourselves spontaneously releasing pain or a deeply held emotion. These experiences tend to happen when we begin to bring awareness to our bodies. Our bodies are home to so many old cellular memories that are simply waiting to be experienced and then released. The teachings of yoga remind us to love what is here. We do this through feeling and experiencing what is within us, and allowing it to release within the space of our openhearted presence.

The beautiful thing about going to yoga is that our teachers remind us to relax, feel, and let go. We are given permission to embody our Being nature. We are given permission to open our chakras and feel the energy and sensitivity that is there. Often, when people teach meditation, they teach it in such a mental way that we do not fully come into our bodies. If we do not step into our bodies fully and energetically, we miss ninety percent of the experience of life. This is why yoga is such a beneficial practice because it awakens us to our Divinity on all levels. Unfortunately, most yoga teachers are not rooted in the awakened perspective or are not trained about the complexity and details of all the chakras or have any clear idea about what it actually means to be free in an enlightened way.

Even without classically trained instructors, though, yoga is greatly beneficial because the practice simply invites us to relax, feel, and embody that which we are. If we are embracing our pain and releasing our past and getting out of our minds, we are heading in the right direction. We will begin to include more and more of ourselves and experience greater levels of Peace and embodiment. This is why the practice itself is so powerful—we all get a taste of this direct experience of our divinity whether we are practicing for the first time or have practiced for years. We will benefit when we practice simply by stepping onto our mats, unhooking from our minds, and coming into ourselves.

Practice: Daily Yoga

Developing a daily yoga routine is essential for increasing the direct experience of awareness. Whether we practice yoga for 10 minutes or 90 minutes each day, our experience of awareness will radically increase.

1. If you have never been to a yoga class, attend a few and find a teacher or practice that resonates with your heart. Learn the major asanas in a series of classes and then bring your practice home and incorporate yoga into your daily spiritual practice. Generally, it is best to practice yoga first and then follow with a seated meditation practice. When you practice in this way, your body will feel more awake and alive, which will help your meditation practice to deepen and become more inclusive. Asana Yoga cannot be taught simply by book, and so it will be beneficial to tour some local yoga studios and discover a

practice which gently challenges you to open in greater ways. Of course, if you live in an area where there are no studios, you can find thousands of free yoga practice videos on the internet through YouTube.

2. Before practicing yoga, take inventory and notice how you feel. After your yoga practice, check in again and see how you are now experiencing yourself. Notice how you feel more alive, awake, and radiant. Let go into this feeling. Give yourself permission to identify fully with this gentle presence that you are—there is no reason to pick up your old habitual self after practicing yoga. Rest in the gentle presence of your heart space.

3. As you practice yoga, be less concerned about trying to cultivate a perfect yoga body and more concerned about the direct experience of true nature. When you practice, you will notice all kinds of physical sensations as you bend and stretch; beyond noticing the physical sensations, notice how your whole energetic body comes alive. Notice the different flows of energy streaming throughout your body. Notice what is happening in each of the seven chakra centers. Feel and experience the quiet presence of the heart, the third eye, and belly. Explore what you are beyond mind, emotion, and body.

Chapter Ten

Retreats

S PENDING TIME IN SILENCE AND GIVING OURSELVES the space to unhook from our intensely busy lives is deeply necessary for those who want to awaken to the experience of true nature. We live in a time where silence is not honored, where it is normal to fill every free moment with work or being engaged in our electronics. But if we want to awaken out of the collective unconscious reality that most of the world lives in, we must be willing to take the time to step out of this self-fabricated busy reality and into the one true Reality. When we commit to retreat practice, we are committed to stepping out of the chaos of our everyday life and into the presence of silence, spaciousness, and true freedom. Retreat time is a time for us to stop, let go, forgive, release, and drop into our unconditional nature. It is a time to be nourished by Grace, a time to deeply connect to the dharma. It is a time for us to truly get to know who we are beyond mind and ego. It is a time to relax and let go into that which is good, true, and beautiful about ourselves.

Sadly, most of us in this modern age believe that we cannot take a break from the lives that we have created. This assumption needs to be deeply examined. Why is it that we think that we cannot take a break from life? If we ask ourselves that question, chances are our mind will come forward and offer many excuses quite quickly: our children, our job, our education, our finances, our relationships... just to name a few. I will not argue that we all have busy lives. But is it actually true that we cannot take a break from them? Is it actually true that we could not take a day, or two days, or four days, or a week, or a month and radically investigate the depth of who and what we are? This question needs not to be asked to our egoic minds (because the answer will be always "no,") but rather, we must ask our hearts. If our hearts want to know a depth of freedom beyond the scope of our minds, then we must be willing to bravely step out of these minds and into the space of silence.

At the busiest time in my life, while being completely overrun with bills, child rearing, and running two businesses, I still made time to meditate every day for at least an hour, meet with my teacher once a week in Satsang for three hours, and also go on retreats. If we want to wake up, our practice must become a way of life. If we want to experience vague or mixed results, then we will allow our practice to be more like a hobby. I imagine that, since you are reading this book, you are interested in what it actually means to be free in this lifetime and not in some distant lifetime. If it is your goal to know yourself as Divine, you must make time to be in silence.

It is not that we "have to" meditate every day, or live like a monk or nun to discover our true nature. The modern day sage, Eckhart Tolle, did not meditate or live like a monk, but he is more of an exception instead of a model we should follow. Anything is possible; the Divine can do anything and wake up in anyone in any moment. There is no guarantee that if we do practice and spend time in silence that we will wake up beyond our egoic identification, but our daily and consistent practice makes us more likely to. If we look at those individuals who have discovered their true nature, the overwhelming majority of them have been serious, dedicated practitioners. It only makes sense that if we want to wake up, we will orient our lives around the investigation of what it means to be free. We can no doubt practice anywhere we are in life, and yet it can be radically transformative to take the time out of our busy schedule to do retreat practice. I have always been amazed at the giant steps forward that individuals make on retreat; no other practice seems more potent than retreat time.

A good Buddhist friend of mine often reminds me that the more retreat practice we do, the greater the chances are that we will create the favorable conditions for waking up. Throughout my life, I have studied with many different individuals who are truly enlightened, and each of them had an intense spiritual practice involving long periods of daily meditation, some form of yoga, and significant retreat time. I have also met some individuals who have glimpsed awakening with no spiritual practice at all. But the individuals whom I have personally met and studied with all have—without exception—made their practice a way of life.

Occasionally, I hear of a rare soul, such as Eckhart Tolle, who did realize his true nature without any practice or study. But again, this is rare, and it would be quite arrogant of us to imagine that we will have the same karma. Many of my teachers have literally spent years of their lives in meditation; they practiced from four to fourteen hours a day for significant periods of their lives. For most of us, this type of practice would be considered insane and outside of the norm of the collective. The very aspiration to be free of our egos is crazy from the perspective of our minds and the collective consciousness. But we must ask ourselves, what type of life do we want to live? One within the realm of our collective insanity or a life of freedom outside of the collective box? If we want to live outside of the box, we must be willing to live in a radically different way.

Retreat time is truly a step out of the collective busyness of our world. If we go on a yoga retreat, we are very likely to become aware of the various places within ourselves where we habitually hold tension and we will be invited to release this tension and discover the brilliance of our energetic body. If we take the time to spend five days in a retreat sitting in meditation and inquiring into the deep questions of our being, there is a good chance we will gain an insightful perspective on the depth of our nature. If we sit for hours and hours on a meditation retreat, there is a good chance we will experience a glimpse of our ultimate nature. This profound experience has the power to radically reorient our lives in unimaginable ways.

The beautiful thing about retreat time is that we are so deeply supported in unhooking from the business of our lives and fully giving ourselves to the investigation of our Divinity. Retreat practice provides a container for us to do this type of work. Usually on retreat there is a teacher who can help guide us in an individual way. And we often have our physical needs taken care of; we are fed and given a place to sleep. We are removed from our normal environment so that we cannot busy ourselves with work, families, to do lists, and other distractions. There are normally rules at retreat, such as maintaining noble silence and not using computers and cell phones, which help to give us the discipline and support to unhook from life. As we slow down, our ego actually begins to fall apart or dissolve because egos thrive on being busy. Without anything to do, our egos begin to have no use and start to settle down. As they do so, we discover what they have been covering up for so long—our original nature. This may come forward in a silent radiant spaciousness, a quiet witnessing, or a gentle luminous presence.

During retreat time we are invited to embody and live from this radiance of that which we are. As we experience this presence more and more and become comfortable with our vibrant nature, we discover that we can live from this place in the "real world." When we go on retreat, we discover that it is possible to live differently; we are encouraged to directly experience our heart, the vastness of the sky, and this moment right here, right now. Yet, when we are in the "real world," we are encouraged to chase the collective dream, always racing here or there while being lost in the rush of our minds. Retreat practice is a welcome opportunity to come home to what we are and to relearn how to live from this space of Beauty and Divinity that we had once forgotten. From this practice of taking the time to rediscover who we truly are, we are able to fully come home to ourselves. With this newfound wisdom in our hearts and greater perspective on life, we can then return to our busy and complex everyday lives with peace, clarity, compassion, and love.

Practice: Commit to Retreat Time

- Examine the busyness of life and notice where you are attached to a schedule which is not of your making. Ask yourself, do I agree with the busyness of the collective norm? Do I want to live in a way where the direct experience of silence is rare? Am I willing to let go of some of my busy schedule in order to discover and know my true nature?

- Find a retreat and sign up for it. Put a retreat on your schedule this year. If there is no local teacher or meditation group offering a retreat, create your own. Spend a day or two or a whole week in nature. Turn the phone off and simply spend time in silence. Commit to a daily retreat meditation and yoga routine. Give yourself the gift of a few days of intense practice. If you can, take a week or a month off from work and simply practice with no distractions. Make this retreat practice a way of life.

- Break away from the collective norm of work and family, and more work and more family, and the trance of consumerism; commit yourself to the spiritual path. Give your time and energy to the path first and foremost. Imagine what your life could be like if you actively choose to step out of the trance state of the collective norm. Imagine reorienting your life in alignment with peace, silence, stillness, and a contemplative atmosphere.

What would you be willing to give up in order to attend a retreat? Are you courageous enough to commit your life to the pursuit of Truth?

- If you have children and cannot get away for long periods of time, can you arrange a mini-retreat? This may involve paying a babysitter or calling on support from your partner or family and getting away just for an afternoon or morning. Can you be creative and take your children to school and take a day off work, just to practice? Can you make time for yourself and your spiritual path? After experiencing a mini-retreat, notice how you respond differently to your children. Perhaps you will find that you respond with more patience and compassion. Notice how taking a break from life is enormously supportive for any parent and creates greater harmony within the family.

- Beyond taking time away for retreat, can you commit to seeing all of life as Divine? Can you step back and see that this whole world is a play of the Divine?

Chapter Eleven

Concentration

T O SUPPORT OUR COMMITMENT OF GIVING OURSELVES fully to the spiritual path, we must be disciplined; we must hold a one-pointed focus and concentration which is unshakable. There is no hope for us on the path of liberation if we are lost following the whims of our monkey minds and fearful egoic nature. We will be lost for years and even perhaps lifetimes without the ability to focus our attention and energy.

Most of us painfully experience this truth within a few weeks after January 1st each year; we have made our New Year's resolutions and then, a few weeks later, we find ourselves again without discipline and without change—often doing exactly the opposite of what we set out to do. Because we all know this experience of being seduced by our very minds, we must cultivate spiritual discipline. Discipline means that we say yes to the truth of our hearts, we say yes to that which is in alignment with our highest nature, and we say no to that which will create more pain, ignorance, and confusion in our lives. This discipline is like a muscle; when we exercise our discipline, we become stronger and are in greater alignment with our truth. When we do not exercise our discipline, we become weak-minded and vulnerable, at the mercy of our monkey minds.

When we have developed the ability to be one pointed, we are less likely to be moved in all directions by our thoughts, emotions, personal conditioning, and our collective conditioning. If we want to be free, we must develop our ability to withstand any storm without bowing down to our fearful or confused minds. When we become one pointed in this way, we can discern what is true and what is false, what is in our heart and what is in our mind, and what is wise and what is foolish.

If we do not have the ability to concentrate—to be one pointed—we will not likely walk very far on the path. We will be confused by our minds, emotions, and conditioning. We will believe the fleeting thoughts of our minds and take them to be the truth of reality instead of seeing them as simply thoughts with no real basis in Reality. We will be carried away by our emotions, and find ourselves lost in the never-ending drama. We will be seduced by the mass thinking of our collective consciousness, chasing the latest trends, grasping at the latest gadget, and swimming in the current insanity of the evening news. But when we actually take the time to learn to concentrate, to deeply be with one thing, we are taking the time to get to know what we are in our true nature, and what we are not. When we take the time to develop the ability to stay focused, we can begin to know what the truth of our being is.

From this space we can actively choose to align with this truth in our everyday lives. If we do not have the ability to concentrate or to be disciplined, we may have an intention to meditate on our true nature for the next hour, and then thirty seconds later we may find ourselves lost gossiping about a friend.

To develop the level of concentration that is necessary to actually progress on the path, we must be willing to learn to meditate and to commit to a meditation practice every day. The path of liberation is not a path for those who are unwilling to radically change their lives; this path is for those who are willing to give everything—our hearts, our attention, our time, and our energy. There is no greater practice to develop concentration, discernment, inner peace, and mindfulness than meditation. Every great wisdom tradition has, at its core, some form of meditation practice. To start, choose a tradition or school of meditation which resonates most with your heart and then commit to this practice.

Practically speaking, if we want to develop the type of discipline and concentration necessary for profound spiritual awakening, we must be willing to sit every day for one hour or more. We can work up to this length of time, but once we become established in our practice, we must be willing to commit to this practice every day. One of the pillars of concentration is attention and the other is commitment. We all have attention, but for most of us our attention is spread all over the place. Many of us can multitask and accomplish many things at once, but not many of us can discover peace and freedom by doing one thing at a time. If you focus on your breath for an hour and are not constantly seduced by your own mind, you will discover a peace that has no end and a freedom as big as the sky—this promise has been told by saints and sages since the beginning of time. It is up to us to discover if this promise is true.

The practice of concentration is fairly basic and similar in almost every tradition. The instructions are to concentrate on your breath, a mantra, or prayer, and then focus on this one point or object and do not move your focus. Your focus should be gentle and openhearted but also firm and disciplined.

This is not a mental activity; it is a *feeling and experiencing activity*. We are feeling into our breath and we are feeling into our hearts and gently holding our attention here.

If you feel tension while you practice meditation, the instructions are to soften your effort and hold a gentle discipline. If you find yourself upset for getting off track, gently come back to the practice without any self-judgment. If judgment arises, we meet ourselves with compassion. We are human and we were given monkey minds, but we can train our minds to be one pointed—it is through this one-pointedness that we are able to know, experience, and abide in our True Nature.

Practice: Meditate on a Candle Flame

Light a candle and sit comfortably. With a gentle gaze, hold your attention on the candle flame. As thoughts arise, let them pass. If you become carried away by the thoughts, bring your attention back to the candle flame. If boredom arises, simply notice the boredom. If fantasies arise, simply notice the arising fantasy, and come back to the candle flame. If thoughts of the past arise, come back to the present and the candle flame.

Notice the aliveness of the present moment. Notice the feeling of the aliveness of your true nature when you are not distracted by the constant story of the mind. Give yourself over to this aliveness, to this Divinity.

Practice: Walking or Yoga Breath Meditation

While walking or doing yoga, place your attention on your breath. Feel into the spaciousness and aliveness of your being while walking or while practicing the asanas. Feel the space, the energy, and the life force in your heart. If you become distracted by thoughts, just come back to the breath and the feeling of aliveness.

Notice the quiet, the silence of the space of presence which you are. Breathe, feel, and experience your nature directly. Rest in this space for some time, even as you continue walking or practicing yoga.

~ *Chapter Twelve* ~

Meditation on the Impermanence of Things

Through the practice of deeply sitting with ourselves, we discover the nature of things, just as they are.

ONE MORNING, I AWOKE FROM MY FROST-COVERED TENT at the base of a mountain and watched as the snow melted and turned into a stream. As I sat in meditation, I watched the impermanence of this world right before my eyes. This massive mountain was slowly being carved and eroded by the movements of glaciers, snow, ice, wind, and rain—these forces of nature slowly were having their way with the mountain. When we sit openheartedly without hiding from the truth of this world, we see that everything in this realm, including us, will fall before this truth of impermanence. This is a truth that no pill, surgery, or facial cream can prevent, despite the billions of dollars that are spent on these things each year. We may slow down the occurrence of wrinkles from forming on our beautiful faces, but make no mistake: impermanence is simply a law of this worldly reality. We see and experience this truth each year as we get older and our bodies begin to slow down and age. We see it in our cars, our electronics, and in our friends and families. Everything will grow or change and eventually turn to dust.

This truth of impermanence is not something we need to struggle against; rather it is something we can embrace, for it has the ability to set us free if we are willing. As I sat longer in meditation, I turned my attention inward and watched as my thoughts and emotions, and my agendas and opinions arose within the space of my mind and then took their death within the same space of my mind. I watched as things that I thought were really important crumble before awareness. All of my great thoughts, all of my beliefs, and all of my stories, came forward and died within this beautiful space of freedom.

Too often, we attach to our identities, beliefs, moods, and emotions and mistake these for what we are. But all of these are simply passing experiences, as humbling as that may sound. In the end, the only thing permanent about each of us is this vast, empty, alive space of our presence.

Practice: Impermanence Meditation

Sit in meditation and watch as a thought arises, and then watch it pass away. Sit still and watch another thought arise and then disappear. Do not become involved with the thoughts, simply watch them come and watch them dissolve into the space of your mind.

You can do this practice for 10 minutes or 2 hours or any length of time in between, but once you decide upon a length of time, be true to your intention.

✳ ✳ ✳

Monks spend years of their lives simply working with this practice of noticing the impermanence of all things. This is a progressive practice. We start simply by watching thoughts come and go. We notice their inherent impermanent nature. We notice how they are unconnected from Reality. When we become stable in this mindfulness practice, we can practice with thoughts and our comments about our thoughts, and with our mental and emotional judgments and deeply held beliefs. We can allow this presence of mindfulness to expand and include our everyday lives.

We can watch as the next thought arises and the tendency to cling to it, get involved with it, analyze it, control it, and now *do nothing*. Now watch both the tendency to micromanage thought and the thought itself falling away. We can also extend this practice to the sensations which arise within us, and the emotions which arise, which are also impermanent. Notice sensations arise and do nothing. Watch them intensify, change, morph, and pass away. Notice an emotion arise and do nothing. Watch it pass away. Experience the freedom in allowing everything to come and go. Experience the tightness and tension in wanting thoughts to stay or go. Experience the tightness and tension when we attach to a thought, believe in it, and get carried away by it. Again and again, experience the freedom of letting everything come and go.

Now reflect upon how everything we think and feel is impermanent. Notice how there is more space within our own self, how our relationship to what we think becomes more spacious, more flexible, and more light-hearted when we see that every thought, emotion, and sensation we have is impermanent.

We can practice this not only in meditation, but also when we have the desire to eat one more cookie or purchase another thing we do not need. We can practice this when we have an agenda to finish writing this section of our book on yoga and our baby is crying and needs our attention; we can let our agenda die. We can let every thought die in the space of impermanence and come into the freedom of the present moment. We can pick up our baby and go for a walk and experience the raindrops falling while carrying our baby down the street.

~ *Chapter Thirteen* ~

Contemplation and Inquiry

C ONTEMPLATION IS THE ART OF DEEPLY REFLECTING upon some aspect of life that we do not fully comprehend. Through this reflective art, we are not necessarily looking to find some great philosophical answer, but rather to experience the Truth directly in this present moment. To step into the space of contemplation is similar to stepping into the space of meditation. It requires both a sense of humility and honesty to admit that our mind does not have all the answers to the majority of our deepest questions. And perhaps if we did have some quick philosophical answers to these questions in our minds, if we are honest, we can admit that deep in our being, *we know that we do not know.*

The great spiritual questions of "Who am I?" or "What is God?" or "What is love?" are questions we have all mentally or philosophically struggled with to no end and require a different type of investigation beyond our mental reasoning. What is required is that we become quiet and open our hearts to a wisdom vastly greater than our small egoic minds. These questions, when asked to our hearts from a place of sincerity, will give birth to a different kind of Truth. Not a truth of reason and philosophy, but a Truth of Divine power in our lives.

This practice of contemplation is not only reserved for questions on the nature of God or our being. Sometimes these questions are more practically related to our everyday lives. If we do not know why we continue to struggle in our personal relationships, we may want to investigate this more deeply. We may choose to become quiet and spend a period of time deeply reflecting on our relationship. We may reflect on our behaviors and the behaviors of our partner. But in order to deeply reflect upon something, we cannot simply employ our minds in the games of the blame and judgment; we must instead look to our hearts. The equanimity and wisdom of the heart is what separates contemplation from simply thinking about something in a psychological or analytical way.

In order to deeply contemplate something, we must first have the attitude of being open—open to seeing and receiving that which we cannot readily see with our minds. When we think about a topic in a mental way, we are using our intellect to solve a problem. But contemplation is quite different in that we are not enlisting our minds to find an answer. Contemplation is not an intellectual activity; it is a willingness to align with the intelligence of Grace to show us something we cannot or do not see with our human minds. That is why when we contemplate something, we begin by letting go of our mentality—our agendas, our preconceived ideas, our beliefs about the past, or hopes for the future. To truly contemplate is to step into the unknown and begin to look at something as if it is the very first time that we are truly seeing it.

In a practical sense, this means we become quiet; we let go of our thoughts and open to our question, to the situation at hand, whatever it may be; we open to what is before us, and simply listen from our heart. We allow our heart to guide us, to speak to us, to teach us that which is unknown to us.

When we open in this way, the universe responds. The universe is silently waiting for us to become sincere and open our hearts to Her wisdom. When we do so, She responds with a movement of Grace. In order for us to receive this Grace, we have to be sensitive, receptive, and quiet. When our answer comes, it will be like a cool breeze or a resonating force within us. When it comes we will know it because it will ring true like a clear bell. This Grace will not come with a big mental argument or emotionality. It will come either like a silent peace or a resonating power which arises out of our heart. Sometimes our answer may come from the lips of another or in some act of physical Grace; we may hear our teacher give us the answer without us asking, or see our answer written on the page of a spiritual book which we just opened, or it may arise from the eyes of our child. How Grace comes to us is ever mysterious, yet the timing is always right and it comes with the force of Truth.

Most of the profound questions we ask in life will only be answered through the space of deep contemplation—through us silently sitting with the unknown. As we sit and open, we may watch our mind struggle or try to come up with a quick solution. However, most mental solutions will not have any depth or power to them—they will be as insecure as our mind is. Ultimately, we will not be satisfied with intellectual answers to our deep questions.

I have been asked countless times, "Why do bad things happen to good people?" I have come to peace with this question in my heart after decades of contemplating this paradox. However, my answer, if given, will not satisfy another. I can give my answer, but unless someone has come into this same space of understanding, it will be just empty words. But this is a good thing; no teacher owns the truth. This truth that we seek is within us, and it is through the doorway of contemplation—through becoming quiet and being open, receiving, and patient, that the truth is revealed.

If we are going to discover the truth deep within our hearts, it will come to us in one of three ways: by Grace, by contemplation, or by inquiry (all of which are really Grace). We cannot make Grace happen, but we can be open to receiving Grace in our lives and be proactive in our relationship with truth. Opening to Grace often involves taking the time to stop and deeply investigate the great questions of life and contemplate the unknown. Closely related to the practice of contemplation is inquiry. Inquiry takes place in the same space of quiet openheartedness, yet is much more assertive in the sense that we actively question our thoughts, beliefs, assumptions, judgments, and experiences. We may inquire: Are the thoughts that I think true? Do I actually know what a thought is or where it comes from? Are my assumptions about life true? How do I feel when I believe this thought or when I act a certain way? Are my emotional reactions true or are they simply egoic defenses which arise from not seeing clearly? Are my experiences in this moment an accurate reflection of the truth? Or are my experiences simply conditioned responses from my conditioned ego?

When we inquire in this way, we find that much of what we think is made up of simply unexamined assumptions. Unfortunately for us, these unexamined assumptions—when streamed together by the movement of our minds—create a virtual reality. We unconsciously believe in this virtual reality, experience suffering as a result, and live a life of delusion, separated from our natural state, which is clear, sane, free, and blissful. The crystal clear presence of our true nature is covered up by our belief in the validity of our thoughts, which fuels our egoic nature. This unconscious identification with our minds is the basic egoic delusion that spirituality attempts to free us from. At the core of egoic delusion is our own belief in our minds. This trance state happens from simply believing a single thought, and then another, and another. These thoughts, strung together, create the illusion of a separate egoic self.

When we believe a simple thought such as "My partner should do the dishes," we can spin ourselves into a total delusion in a matter of seconds. As a counselor, I have spent an enormous amount of time listening to the outrageous thoughts of my clients. As an avid meditator, I have spent literally years of my life, watching observing, and being fooled by my own delusional thoughts. If we look at the previous example thought of "My partner should do the dishes," and allow this thought to continue unexamined, the accompanying thoughts may be: "They don't do the dishes because they don't care about me. All they care about is themselves! They don't ever do anything nice for me!! I am the only one who is doing anything in this relationship!!! If they loved me, they would do the dishes and I would not have to ask!!!! If only I was with someone else, who treated me better..."

The point of inquiry is not so much to come up with an answer or solution in our minds, but instead to come into the space beyond ego— into the direct experience of Reality. We may come to one mental conclusion while beginning our investigation, but in the end we will come into the space of the direct experience of peace and freedom. With inquiry, we are not asking our mind for an answer; this would simply be the realm of thinking. With inquiry we are asking our heart, we are asking God, Life, the Universe, and we are waiting for the direct experience of the answer. Take, for example, the question, "Who am I *before thought arises*?" There is no mental answer we can give ourselves which will suffice. When we ask this question, we step into the space of Silence, beyond our thinking mind, beyond our egoic nature. We step into the space of our awake, alive, mysterious presence.

We can use inquiry in any moment, whether we are contemplating the deep nature of what we are or we can use inquiry to look into why we find ourselves confused in an egoic trance. For example, if we find ourselves angry, we can inquire into what we are angry about. We can ask, "Is what I am thinking absolutely true?" And by *absolutely true*, we mean *true* in the sense that our thoughts are a direct reflection of Reality. In truth, no thought is a direct reflection of Reality, for no thought (or book) can contain the direct experience of Now. For example, we can ask our hearts a question about the thoughts we are having about our relationship. We can ask, "Is it true that because my partner does not do the dishes that they do not love me?" When our heart answers the question, we see that no, this is not true. We were getting carried away in our virtual reality.

Often, students come to me with the belief that life is unfair. But we can question this thought by asking, "Do I know with total certainty that life is unfair?" Of course we do not, because we cannot see the whole picture—from the mind of God. In a relative sense, yes, life can be fair or unfair. According to our egoic nature, we interpret things as good and bad and right and wrong. But from the perspective of the mind of God, we really do not know why this or that is happening. When we are seeing life through the lens of our egoic nature, we cannot see the strings of karma, or how painful difficult events lead us to grow in compassion, understanding, and unconditional love. Inquiry helps us to step out of our relative mind and into a greater mind. It does this by breaking down the basic unconscious assumptions that we hold so close to us.

For something to be "the truth" in an absolute way, there has to be total certainty. No thought can live up to this measure, for all thoughts are relative, and are not actually the thing itself. All thoughts are reflections about some thing or symbols representing something, but not the thing itself. We can talk about God all day, but the word or thought "God" is nothing in comparison to God Itself. Therefore, anything we think is simply not the absolute truth. This will always be revealed to us if we take a moment to inquire into it. We can think one thousand thoughts about our partner or our parents and become completely carried away in a virtual reality. But none of these thoughts are true; they are simply biased reflections and passing mental symbols in our minds. How often have we worked ourselves up in some terrible story about someone only to find that our story is only just that—a story with no basis in reality? When we discover that our story is simply a story, we are seeing clearly. We can then allow ourselves to truly see our partners and the world without any lens of projection, judgments, or labels. As we see and experience life in this way without a lens to distort, we become closer to the truth, to Reality.

The act of inquiry destroys the stronghold that our thinking mind has over us. When the mind begins to crumble in this way, what we discover is the direct experience of presence—our presence, the presence of those around us, and the presence of Life Itself. We can investigate into this right now if we are willing. Take any thought and ask, "Is this true? Do I know this with total certainty?" When the answer "No" arises, bring your attention to the quiet and stillness which is here when you let go of your egoic identification and attachment to this thought.

Our mind begins to lose its grip upon us when we admit that we do not know anything for certain. In a sense, through inquiry, our mind is forced to admit defeat. When the mind finds itself defeated, we discover the quiet peace that is here in every moment. This presence is always here, yet we miss it because we are busy living in the land of the known—the land of what we think we know to be true. All of our thoughts, beliefs, and opinions about life, all of our mental and emotional chatter distracts us from experiencing the freedom of our very presence. Through questioning our thoughts, we cut through this distraction of mind and see it for what it is—arising movements of conditioned thinking with no inherent reality. What we are left with is our direct experience of the Peace out of which all of life arises.

Practice: Self Inquiry

1. Sit quietly and ask your heart (not your mind) and *feel deeply* into the question, "Who Am I?"

2. Experience the answer. Experience the silence, the quiet, the aliveness. Then rest in this experience. Give yourself full permission to know this as your own self.

3. If you become distracted by or identified with a thought, feeling, or sensation, again ask, "Who Am I?" Again, experience the answer.

4. Allow this experience to lead and guide you. And allow this direct experience of yourself to be the groundless ground where you plant your feet in Reality.

Chapter Fourteen

Beginner's Mind, Never-Ending Study, and Vigilance

D ESPITE ALL OF OUR SPIRITUAL PRACTICES, growth, and realizations, our egoic tendencies are strong and have an amazing ability to resurrect themselves over and over again. Therefore, it is wise to root ourselves in the attitudes of *beginner's mind, never-ending study,* and *vigilance.* These three attitudes will protect us from pride, arrogance, ignorance, and confusion.

Many times on the spiritual path I experienced amazing states of consciousness and even powerful realizations, and yet I can humbly admit that after some period of time, I once again found myself in the grips of human confusion. No matter who we are and no matter how enlightened we think we may be, we can and will fall on our knees again and again. Countless spiritual teachers, saints, and sages have proclaimed amazing realizations and amassed great followings only to one day find themselves again very much confused by their own humanity.

This is not because they were inherently bad teachers or somehow psychologically wrong; this is because they are in human form, and while we are in human form we will always be continually evolving. And evolution is mostly a messy process. Everyone and all beings on this Earth are growing and evolving—for this is an evolutionary world. Knowing this, it is wise to maintain a beginner's mind. Beginner's mind means we become rooted in a humility that knows and accepts that we do not know what to do in most circumstances, and admits we do not know all the answers. We see the value in committing to continually studying the great scriptures, such as the Bible, The Bhagavad Gita, and Yoga Sutras of Patanjali; the writings of modern sages and teachers, such as Sri Aurobindo, Ramana Maharshi, Adyashanti, and Paramahansa Yogananda; as well as writings on modern psychology (which did not exist at the time of the Buddha), from great minds such as Carl Jung and Peter Levine. Furthermore, we must acknowledge the great value in engaging in our own therapy and shadow work. Humility reminds us to examine our lives—our thoughts, our speech, our actions, and our shadow (the unconscious aspects of self that we normally do not see). Shadow work often requires the help of a therapist, skilled practitioner, or teacher to point out that which is hidden within us. This is one of the main reasons why great teachers— as well as individuals like you and I—often fall from grace on the path; there are more healing and integration needed in the realm of our psychological nature and shadow.

Buddhism has often been cited as the first psychology, but even the Buddha's understanding of the mind did not include what Carl Jung later discovered about the shadow, inner child, and the wound. Later, Peter Levine brought forth great understanding and techniques on how to work with trauma and how the body stores pain in the cellular memory. Our shadow, wound, and trauma effectively eclipse or veil our Divine nature; this is why it is important to study both the ancient scriptures and modern wisdom. Not only are we evolving as individual human beings, but our understanding is also evolving and growing with us. Beginner's mind is the attitude of openness to continual growth on the path. And so, we are open to ancient wisdom as well as modern teachings, insights, and therapeutic techniques on how to heal, integrate, embody, and awaken to the fullness of what we are.

In order to support our attitude of beginner's mind and our continual ongoing examination of ourselves and this life, we need to possess or develop vigilance. Vigilance is the ability to never let our guard down. This does not mean that we live behind egoic walls or live a life of continual fighting, or that we are neurotically tense and continually judging or analyzing ourselves. It means that we openheartedly surrender our egoic tendencies—our thoughts, our beliefs, and our emotions—each moment they arise. It also means we are open to feedback and to receiving support along the way. Many spiritual seekers are too proud to ask for help, seek out therapy, or examine their shadow. Vigilance is the strength to look into the unconscious mind and humbly acknowledge where we struggle and where we need help or support. This does not mean that we fight with our mind, try to destroy it, or try to control it. It simply means that, as our humanity arises, we meet it continually with wisdom, with Peace, and with Love. If we fail to do this... if we become arrogant and prideful of where we are on the path, we are sure to fall because we cannot "serve two masters" as Jesus once said. It is wise to accept that we are human and know that as long as we are human we will be growing. It is our ongoing invitation to continually surrender that which is less than to that which is Greater than. In response to the question, "How long must we surrender?" the great Indian sage, Papaji, replied, "until our very last breath."

Practice: Beginner's Mind Inquiry

Starting in beginner's mind, contemplate the following questions:

- Am I proud of my spiritual practices, achievements, and realizations? Do I consider myself a better student, yoga teacher, or meditator than others? Do I feel as if I am more important, more advanced, or more accomplished than others?

When I am prideful or arrogant, do I feel closer and more unified with Life, or more separate and alone?

- Do I repeatedly find myself arguing and defending myself? If so, can I ask myself, what am I defending?

- Am I free to fail, to make mistakes, and grow? If not, am I afraid of being human, of being humble?

- Am I open to learning from everyone and everything? Or am I stuck in egoic pride and divisiveness? Can I see that the entire universe is alive and teaching me? Can I see that Life is teaching me in every moment through pain, heartache, praise, blame, hope, and fear? Can I see that everything in life is here to open and teach me?

- Am I committed to continual practice and continual examination of my ego? Or do I become easily bored and distracted by life? Do I practice each day? Do I make my spiritual life a priority? How deep is my commitment to the Truth, to my path?

- Have I surrendered every aspect of my ego over to something greater?

~ Chapter Fifteen ~

Discerning Wisdom

I F WE WANT TO AVOID CAUSING UNNECESSARY PAIN for ourselves and others in this world, we must practice some form of discerning wisdom. This means that we must be able to discern which thoughts, words, and actions will cause harm and which will cause peace. There are countless texts written on morality and ethics that can help to guide us in regard to our thoughts, behaviors, and actions, but in general we can simply ask ourselves a few basic questions and discern a clear sense of wisdom: Is this action wholesome? Will these words create harmony? Is what I am thinking true? Is this plan of my mind based in Love? Am I speaking the truth? Am I lying to myself or others?

Most of us learned what was right and wrong by the time we finished kindergarten. We learned to tell the truth. We learned to not take that which does not belong to us. We learned how to share. We learned not to harm another physically, mentally, or emotionally. We even learned some degree of appropriate boundaries in relationships with others. However, most of us have not yet mastered our minds and do not know how to work with our emotions or even possess a fair degree of emotional intelligence. Because of this, today—just like when we were in kindergarten—we are still learning how to live without harming ourselves or others. This is why we need to develop a strong discerning wisdom. We must have the discipline to stop our minds from creating havoc in our lives and in the lives of others.

In order to stop our minds from creating havoc and karma, it is important to have a few things in place first:

- ✓ We must know that we are not our minds, but rather, we are the *observer* or *witness* of our thinking minds, emotional nature, and physical form.

- ✓ We must have an ability to see the mind clearly for what it is and have an understanding of how and why the mind and emotional nature habitually operate the way they do.

- ✓ We must have a discipline which can stop the unhelpful egoic or neurotic aspects of our mind once we have seen it, and the wisdom to know how to proceed from the heart.

- ✓ We must develop a deep capacity to rest as awareness in order to clearly see what the mind is up to. This means that we must have the ability to unhook from our minds and be able to observe what is arising within our consciousness.

Anyone can become aware simply by taking a step backwards into *the space* out of which all thoughts, emotions, sensations, and sounds arise. We can close our eyes and become aware of the sounds around us. We can notice the sounds arise and then fall away. We can notice a thought coming into our consciousness and then fall away. We can notice an emotion arise and the story that comes with it; we can notice the tendency to believe in this story, cling to or defend it, and we can notice this all fall away. We can notice sensations arise and fall away. The more we practice being aware, the greater our capacity will be to be free of that which arises within us, and to discern what will cause harm and what will create peace.

Most of us, though, have monkey minds and cannot sustain clear awareness for more than a few seconds. To aid in this we must practice daily and diligently, and also understand how and why the mind operates the way it does. When we know how and why it operates in a habitually guarded, defended, or pleasure-seeking manner, we are less likely to be fooled and pulled back into it.

If we stop and observe our egoic mind clearly, we will see that it has two primary movements: moving toward that which is pleasurable, and moving away from that which it does not like or is painful. These primitive movements of mind—"I want" and "I don't want"—drive the actions of the entire animal kingdom as well as most of humanity. This primitive drive, when lacking wisdom, can create enormous pain in our world.

As a father of a six-year-old, there are times when I want her to behave a certain way when we are at church or while she is playing with her friends. If I have a sense of compassion for who she is and how old she is, I can accept it if she does not immediately act the way I am asking. With mindfulness I can be patient, even if her behavior is frustrating. Although, if I do not have any emotional intelligence—knowledge of my habitual emotional nature and what I am feeling at any given moment—I may unconsciously snap at her or repeat how my father parented me (sometimes with fear and intimidation). With discernment, I can notice my frustration, refuse to act on it, and instead breathe, feel, let go, and accept what is. Many of us, however, do not have emotional intelligence and we simply become slaves to whatever feelings that arise within us. But with emotional intelligence, we learn to observe our thoughts and emotions, understand why they arise, and how some emotions belong to our ancestors. It is common for us to repeat the emotions and behavioral patterns of our parents and ancestors when we are unaware of our inner psychology.

Similarly, many of us know the experience of unconsciously acting upon desire. For example, some of us have eaten an entire ice cream cone or bag of candy or box of cookies before remembering that we were on a diet! Many of us crave sugar or junk food and just eat what "tastes good," while ignoring the negative effect these foods may have on our bodies. A basic discriminating discernment helps to remind us to be aware of what we feed ourselves, how it makes us feel, and what food and drink can do to our body. When we consciously choose to exercise and eat a healthy whole food diet, our body tends to feel good and operate at optimum health. But if we just eat what we find pleasurable in the short term, we tend to suffer health consequences in the long term. When we live in a way that is unconscious, simply seeking pleasure and avoiding pain, without any objectivity or emotional intelligence, we will experience short-term pleasure and long-term pain. Discernment turns the table upside down on the basic egoic program of seeking pleasure and avoiding pain. Discernment is the skill to see the big picture, and not give into immediate gratification or avoidance. Most of us do not know how to be with that which is temporarily uncomfortable in order to experience long-term happiness. The skill of discernment brings into question, "*What do I truly want? Do I want ice cream and to satisfy my craving for sugar or do I want health? Do I want to shut my kid up or do I want to raise a healthy child and family?*"

As we step back from our own minds, we see that our very minds are mostly movements of habit: the habit toward seeking short-term pleasure and away from pain. But when we connect with our wise hearts, we can see that chasing short-term pleasure and avoiding short-term pain often leads to long-term pain and suffering. With a little humility, we can take a look and see how habitually addicted we are to seeking pleasure and avoiding pain. Just try spending an entire day in silence, without eating snacks, and without having a mobile device or computer to surf the internet. When we are deeply honest with ourselves, many of us find it hard just to simply be silent and alone, with no work or device to distract us from what we are feeling inside. How many of us are truly happy enough to sit outside on a warm summer night and do nothing but *be the quiet radiance of being*?

Most of us have not yet progressed to a point where we are happy *just as we are*. Instead, we have spent our lives unconsciously seeking short-term pleasure and avoiding pain at all costs. If this is us, we must learn the skill of mindfulness—the ability to *witness* our mind. From this space we can then observe what our mind is doing. Often, this dance of our unconsciousness becomes entangled in games of lying, manipulating, sneaking, and justifying our actions so that we can have more short-term pleasurable experiences while hiding, avoiding, or defending against life. With awareness and understanding, we can see what our mind is up to and see that *we have a choice* whether to follow it or not. With discipline, we can stop these habitual movements and choose to be kind, generous, and compassionate to ourselves in healthier ways. In the heat of the moment, when we choose to compassionately breathe into the pain, we may experience short-term anxiety, loss, or grief. But as we learn to breathe, feel, and experience what is here now, and then naturally let go, we begin to discover true, lasting happiness.

Practice: Inquiring for Wisdom

You can ask yourself a few basic questions and come to a clear sense of wisdom in relationship to your life:

- Am I awake and aware, or am I lost in my egoic nature?

- Is this action wholesome?

- Will these words create harmony and peace?

- Is what I am thinking true?

- Is this plan of my mind based in Love?

- Am I speaking the truth? Am I lying to myself or others?

- What is true in my Heart?

- Is this plan of my mind based in Love or in thought, an emotion, or a hidden agenda?

- How does my inner judge or critic show up within my spiritual path? Do I speak harshly to myself? Do I attack and judge the way I practice? Am I inwardly mean to myself?

- Do I love myself? Am I inwardly kind to myself?

- Do I catch myself unconsciously moving through life? If so, how and when do I become unconscious?

- In what areas of my life could I benefit from greater mindfulness or emotional intelligence?

Chapter Sixteen

The Law of Karma

OUR THOUGHTS, SPEECH, AND ACTIONS AFFECT ourselves, others, and our state of mind—this is the law of karma. In a practical sense, we know that what we do has an impact on the basic reality of ourselves and others. This is common sense, but it is something that many of us forget when we are in the grips of our egoic minds. When we reflect upon our lives, we find that we have done many things that we are not proud of. We do many things out of greed, anger, sadness, or manipulation. In the moment, we may feel justified even if we are in fact quite deluded by our egoic nature. Upon reflection, we can see how much pain we cause when we act from our egoic nature. To be able to see our thoughts, speech, and actions in the heat of the present moment requires that we be mindful—able to see our unfolding humanity from our hearts. To actually stop and change our behaviors takes sincerity from our hearts. We may try to change from the strength and discipline of our minds, but in the end, if this change is to be true, it must come from the sincerity of our hearts.

When we think about the consequences of our actions, we may think, "I want to be good so that good things happen to me." But this perspective is based on wanting pleasure and fearing negative consequences. However, when we come into our hearts and ask, "How shall I meet the world?" The answer is always with love, with peace, with generosity and kindness—not because it is the "right" thing to do, or because we will be rewarded, but because this is the nature of the Heart.

The Buddha's view on karma was that when our actions are pure, we experience happiness, generosity, love, and wisdom, which leads one to happiness. The attitudes of greed, hatred, and delusion lead to suffering. From a place of clear seeing, we may ask ourselves, which qualities of mind are we cultivating? What is the motivation behind our actions? Before we speak or act or think, we must look at what our motivations are. Are our motivations a movement or game of our egoic mind grasping at an unwholesome desire? Or are our actions arising out of the goodness of our hearts?

When we have developed the capacity of mindfulness, we are able to see what the mind is up to and we can steer ourselves toward that which is wholesome. When we walk toward that which is wholesome, we will experience wholesome states of mind. When we walk toward that which is greedy or aggressive or deluded, we will experience those same states of mind. Most of us tend to forget this. We forget that when we lie, we feel bad. When we scheme, we feel like a schemer, and when we are aggressive, we feel like hell. We tend to forget this because our egoic minds are loud and seductive and they act in arrogant and selfish ways.

The ego is a movement of arrogance and self-centeredness. The primary aim of the ego is one's own benefit. This is a helpful trait if we are fighting for our survival. However, most of us rarely experience a true moment of fighting for our survival in this modern age, but we continue to be ruled by an egoic mind which thinks that it is. Even though we have minds that tend to be selfish and overreactive, we can tame the mind through meeting it with loving kindness and gently applying the Buddha's teaching on karma: If we want to experience goodness in our lives, we will redirect our minds toward that which is naturally within our heart. We will choose to express our Beauty, our Peace, our Kindness, and our Generosity. As we do so, our unmanifest essential nature becomes manifest—it becomes our experience in our daily lives. And as it does, our suffering diminishes and happiness becomes a way of being.

Practice: Before You Speak or Act

- Which qualities of mind am I cultivating?

- What is the motivation behind my actions?

- Are my motivations a movement or game of my egoic mind grasping at an unwholesome desire? Or are my actions arising out of the goodness of my heart?

- Will this thought, speech, or action lead to greater happiness or greater suffering?

- Am I looking for short-term happiness while creating long-term suffering?

- Am I creating Peace or am I creating pain?

- What would my Heart do in this situation right now?

Chapter Seventeen

The Direct Experience of the Heart

I F WE ARE GOING TO FULLY BE ALIVE TO THIS LIFE—if we are going to experience the ever-present beauty and divinity of this world, we must choose to live in the here and now. When most of us first hear this teaching, we interpret it through the lens of our habitual egoic minds. Ironically, being mindful has little, if anything, to do with our thinking minds. Since most of us do not know this in the beginning, we often try to think our way into a state of mindfulness.

To truly be present, we have to experience life through the eyes of our heart. This is a radically different experience than having a mentally based relationship to life. If I become present to my baby in a mentally focused way, I may attentively meet her needs. I may wonder what she is thinking and wanting next. I may get her another toy and try to make her smile. These are all good ways to attend to my child and doing these things may make me a good parent. However, if this is the only level on which I relate to my baby, then I will be missing something quite profound—I will be missing the direct experience of who my child is. If I only relate to my child in a mental way, I will miss the beauty pouring out of her eyes, the radiance of her presence, and the divinity of her heart.

In order for me to directly experience this moment from the open nature of the heart, I must bring my attention—my awareness—into my own heart and begin to experience life from this space of presence. When I sit with my baby and hold her in my arms, I can feel the radiance of her heart. I experience the light and glow coming off her crown chakra at the top of her head. I feel her energy merge with my own radiance and I experience an ever-present love and unity with her. This is not an emotional experience or a mental one—it is a direct experience of her Divinity. This experience of Divinity is not limited to the relationship of a father and his baby; we can live this experience with everyone—and all of life. We can meet our partners, parents, families, and our dogs in this way. We can meet the sky, the ocean, the trees, and the garbage dump from this space. No one and no thing exists outside of this space. Our egoic minds are the only thing that creates this division within us.

If we want to live beyond these divisions that our egoic minds fabricate, we must be open to experiencing life differently than we have in the past. All that is required is a willingness to live—to experience life—from the space *beyond* mind and ego. We do this by taking a step back out of our egoic nature and into the space which is here in every moment. We choose to see and experience life without a filter or lens of our past perceptions. We choose to directly experience the energy and the aliveness of everything around us.

In this moment, my mind may want to finish writing this book and my emotions may be dwelling on writing deadlines, but I have the conscious choice available to instead fully be with what is here now. I can become frustrated because I want to continue writing but have a little baby who wants my attention, or I can let go of my personal agenda and kiss my baby's head while she radiates love from her being. When I give myself permission to directly experience life through the heart, I experience aliveness, oneness, unity, and spaciousness—which are all here in every moment—and the temporal experiences of life, such as the radiance of my baby's wide open heart as she sits here in my arms.

Many passing experiences may come and go in the space of my presence, but the spaciousness, oneness, and experience of unity will remain as long as I continue to experience life through my heart. In this moment, my baby is now crying because she wants milk from her mother, yet the spaciousness of my mind is still here even while the thought arises to get her to her mother as quickly as possible. My egoic nature even may complain because it wants her to stop crying. But again, these are passing thoughts. I can take care of her needs, see the complaints of my mind, and continue to be free as long as I do not identify with or believe in my complaints. I can see the complaints as empty thoughts, and take the action required to meet my daughter's needs and remain rooted in my true nature. As long as I am rooted in my heart, I am free from my passing thoughts and judgments. But as soon as I identify with my thoughts—as soon as I believe in them fully and allow these thoughts to define this moment—I become contracted and entranced by ego. When I step away from the space that I am and re-identify with my mind, I become small and separate. But if I am willing to stay open with my child, I will continue to feel and experience the oneness with her and with life, and can now take care of her needs from a space of true love and unity, not from a place of separation.

Again, it is not that there is anything wrong with living only from the limited perspective of our mental minds or our emotional nature; it is just that when we do, we are entranced by our thoughts and emotions. As a result, our experience will feel inherently limited and separate because we are experiencing life through this lens of a separate egoic mind. To be free of this separation, it requires that we choose to be greater than our limited egoic sense of self. Each moment, the choice arises where we can choose to meet life from our egoic nature or instead meet life from the openness of our hearts. What we choose determines our experience of life and our state of consciousness.

We must be careful not to misunderstand this teaching. Many of us assume that if we are living from the openhearted space of our being that we will be eternally showered with bliss and never experience anything uncomfortable. In some spiritual communities, there is such a heavy emphasis on experiencing bliss that there is no room for the human experience of being in pain. But pain is part of life and no amount of transcendence can ever get us off the hook from being human. It is easy to assume that as long as we are experiencing spaciousness and oneness that our experience will feel good all the time, but this is not always the case.

To truly be unified with all of life means that we experience everything—not only the joyous and blissful aspects of life, but we will experience everything within us and all around us, including the good, the bad, and the ugly. This is one of the great paradoxes of unity consciousness, of oneness; we experience the great non-division of all things—good and bad, right and wrong, pain and pleasure, praise and blame—all of which are welcome within the space of what we are. True freedom, true love has no boundaries and welcomes all. This does not mean that we will eternally feel good. If we are open, we will experience openness, and if pain is present, we will also experience this pain, for love does not reject that which is within us. To be free in this way requires us to be open and courageous enough to fearlessly embrace all that arises from the radical openness of the heart.

Practice: Deeper Than the Emotional Heart

Part 1: Getting to Know the True Heart

The emotional heart lives on the surface of our chest, while the True Heart is located underneath the emotional heart, deeper and closer toward the spine.

1. Take the backward step into the space of awareness.

2. Unhook from egoic identification with thought and emotion and simply witness the thinking mind and emotional mind.

3. Notice how the thinking mind feels and operates, the subtle tension, the habitual thoughts, and judgments, etc.

4. Next, notice how the emotional nature or emotional heart feels. Notice the emotional feelings in the heart and belly, such as anger, resentment, sadness, fear, or subtle tension. Simply breathe and witness the feelings while gently inviting everything to relax and be held in a state of love. Do this as long as it takes.

    This is an important step; if you try to skip over this process, you will never discover your True Heart. Please breathe, feel, open, and experience until your body lets go of whatever you are holding.

5. Next, invite awareness to journey deeper inward and discover the True Heart. Feel the quiet tender space within. Notice the strength and purity of being which is your Nature. Breathe here for five minutes or so. Notice how the True Heart feels in comparison to the emotional heart. Rest here.

Part 2: Eyes of the World

6. Now, imagine that you have eyes looking out from your True Heart.

7. Notice how your experience of life changes when you see life from this nondual space.

8. Notice what it is like to see the world new, fresh, and alive.

9. How do you respond to life differently when you see the world through the lens of Love and unity?

10. What is it like not to be a human character called "me," but rather to be the Eyes of the World?

11. See and experience the Beauty of Life in a new and profound way.

Chapter Eighteen

Silence

THERE IS A DEEP VALUE IN SPENDING TIME IN SILENCE. When we take the time to be in silence, we are taking the time to allow Life to show us who we are beyond our egoic nature. If our egoic nature has nothing to say and nothing to do, it quickly loses the wind from its sails. It is difficult for an ego to maintain its authority within us if we are being silent for an extended period of time. When we are silent, we are choosing to step outside of our habitual way of being. We are choosing to say "no" to our neurotic sense of self and to spend our time discovering our true self.

We are also taking the time to allow Life to open us to something greater than our own habitual perspective. As we open in this way, our relationship with our self grows and becomes something quite greater than what we knew ourselves to be. Our relationship with the Divine also grows because we are taking the time to listen to Her voice speak to us. Sometimes She speaks to us through our hearts or from a quiet place of truth within our minds. Sometimes She reveals great truths to us from the very places which scare us—the places we have been avoiding or ignoring. As we listen in this deep way, we liberate that which once bound us. Yet, as long as we are busy in our current dramas, we will never find this depth of Truth within us. It is by being silent that we open this doorway.

Every spiritual practice has a connection with Silence at its core. It is through this doorway of silence that we come in contact with our heart, with the Truth, with that which is greater than our limited egoic nature. Many of us, however, are afraid of silence, for it is where the ego's authority is challenged and seen through. When we are silent, we become honest about what we are really feeling under all the mental chatter. From this space we have the opportunity to heal, to let go, to awaken and discover something deeper than even our deeply personal emotions. This deeper something is the doorway to the heart, to our Divine presence. If we truly desire to step into the fullness of what we are, we must be comfortable with silence—for silence is our very nature.

Practice: Discovering Silence

- What is here before sound arises?
- What is here in every moment?
- What is the sound of awareness?
- What is the sound of your own presence?

Practice: Allowing this Silence to Teach You

- When you become deeply quiet, what does this silence want to communicate with you?
- What does this silence have to show you?
- How does this silence speak to you?
- How does this silence move through your presence?

Practice: Spending time in silence

With no phone or electronics:

1. Spend an hour at dawn or dusk, simply sitting outside witnessing the sky. Notice how vast the sky is. Notice how the

very nature of your mind is like the sky. Do not focus on the thoughts in your mind but rather the space of your mind. Notice how the sky holds the clouds, the trees, the birds, the ocean, etc.

2. In the same way, notice how your true mind is empty and free and also holds your thoughts, emotions, and identity.

3. Rest here and experience how vast your nature is when you are silent and unhooked from egoic identification.

Practice: Walking Silence

1. Put everything down and simply go outside and walk with no agenda but to just walk and be the silence. Resist the temptation to think, listen to your phone or music or fill the air with anything. Simply walk without thought.

2. Breathe in and breathe out. Feel the spaciousness of the sky. Be no one—no character, no identity. Let go of all roles, simply walk and be the Silence. Feel your heart, open and free. Let the mind be silent and vast like the sky.

3. If you find yourself thinking again, simply unhook from thought and come back to the direct experience of Silence— walking Silence.

Practice: Spend a Day or More in Sacred Silence

Again with no phone or electronics, no books, or entertainment of any sort or distraction, spend an entire day in sacred Silence.

1. Make a personal retreat or pilgrimage away from home where you will spend a day or more in silence. Visit a park, go camping, hiking, visit the forest, mountains, ocean, or desert

and simply go and be empty and free like the sky. Give yourself permission to do nothing but simply be. Make the vow to not look at your phone or check in with work—trust that life will be just fine without your continual engagement. Give yourself full permission to dive deep into the experience of silence.

2. Notice how you feel when you first step into the silence. It is normal to feel anxious, or attached to your phone (it is best to leave it behind), work schedule, or to compulsive doing. Unhook from all the demands of modern life and go walk around, hike, lay in the grass and be with the sky—be with the hugeness of your consciousness. Be with the stillness of nature. *Be no one and no thing.* Just be.

3. At first this may feel unsettling, but stay with the silence... drink it in. Receive the healing energy of the sky and of nature. Receive the nourishing freedom of not having to do or perform. Give yourself the freedom to live beyond the limited nature of your egoic identity or character.

4. Notice how your body, mind, and emotional nature deeply relax the more time you spend in silence. Rest here in this space.

Be this space—silent awake and aware of your own Divinity.

Chapter Nineteen

Grace

MANY OF US ON THE SPIRITUAL PATH HAVE NO relationship with Grace—the movement of God in one's life. After years of teaching, this continues to absolutely confuse and shock me. How can we be on the path and not have an intimate relationship with the movement of God in our lives? In our materialist and scientific world, many of us have forgotten that there is such a thing as Grace or that we have a Creator. Our culture and educational systems have decided to only value the cold material facts of this world, completely missing the overwhelming Beauty and Divinity pouring out of every living thing. We have valued science and stripped our hearts of a deep connection with our Creator. This is by far one of the greatest sins that we could commit against ourselves and our world. It is not that there is anything wrong with scientific knowledge; I am in no way dismissing the value of science and reason from which we have gained so much. We would have a very difficult time functioning in this world without them. But we do ourselves a great disservice when we make science our god and dismiss all else as superstition or nonsense. Within the world of the Divine there is room for everything, including science. After all, who is it that made the very laws of science and this material reality? However, in the world of science there is very little room for God. This shows our supreme human arrogance—that we imagine that we know more than our Creator.

For those of us who are tired of trying to figure out the ineffable with only our rational minds, we can instead be willing to know God through the experience of our heart.

To open to Grace is to develop a relationship with our Creator and our own Divinity. It is to open our hearts and say, "Yes, I want to have a direct and personal relationship with God." It is the humility to know that our hearts are good and worthy of God's love. It is to admit that our hearts are not separate from God and to acknowledge that our very hearts are the direct doorway to God. Humility is necessary because we must be willing to step out of the arrogance of our minds and into the quiet presence of our hearts if we are going to receive something much greater than ourselves.

We can experience Grace in countless ways. We may become quiet and gently pray or ask God a question, and then wait for the answer. We may hear a voice, receive a vision, or simply *feel* the answer come in a movement of light, warmth, or peace. We may simply set the intention in the morning to open to Grace and see what comes. We may experience a descent of energy into our heart, mind, or body. We may walk down the street and become flooded with light. Or a stranger may smile to us in the perfect moment when we are having a tough day. The movement of Grace has no boundaries and no limitations.

We may even be used by God to *be the Grace*. My little baby has touched the lives of so many, by just her presence alone. It is hard for me to walk across a parking lot without someone stopping and telling me how "her smile made their day." While walking down the street, faces light up when they see my baby pass by. The movement of Grace is such a mystery; we have no idea of when or how it may come. This mystery can radically change our life if we allow it. What is required of us is to be open, willing, and humble enough to receive this movement which is continually being showered upon us.

Practice: Open to Grace

1. Sit quietly and invite awareness to come into the space of the heart.

2. In a humble or childlike way, invite the presence of God to come into you.

3. Sit quietly and listen in your heart. Notice how you feel when you call upon God.

4. Notice if there comes a gentle stream of Light, Warmth, Peace, Love, or other gentle experiences and sensations flowing into your body and energetic field. Be open to the way God shows up in your experience.

5. Relax, breathe, feel, and open to what is coming.

6. Smile. Know and trust that you are a child of God.

If you sit and open but do not immediately feel the Grace of God enter you, do not become frustrated. *Do not expect to find the experience of Grace in your thinking mind.*

Continue opening and trusting and listening for this Grace to come. It is always here but sometimes we are unconsciously blocked in our heart. Continue praying for God's Grace to enter you, and move on to the next practice.

Practice: Examining Your Relationship With God

Sometimes when we practice opening to Grace, we do not feel anything because we have unconsciously placed a wall between us and God. Let us examine this.

Sit quietly and get in touch with the quiet space of your heart. Sit for some time with each of the following questions:

- What is my relationship with God? Have I closed any doors to God?

- Have I replaced God with Science or reason?

- Am I afraid to acknowledge God because it brings forth my inherent vulnerability?

- Do I not acknowledge God because I view God as a concept of religion or religious ignorance? Could it be possible that there are concepts about God *and* an actual experience of God?

- Am I angry at God because I view the world (God's creation) as a dangerous place and do not understand that if God is love, why God would create a world with so much suffering?

- Am I willing to forgive God for creating a world in which suffering exists and again open my heart to the mystery of God?

- Can I acknowledge that perhaps I do not understand God's Intelligence, and that this world is a world of both evolution and growth, and that we often grow through suffering?

- Am I willing to speak to God and share my hopes, needs, and fears? Am I willing to ask God for support?

- Am I willing to trust that there is a greater plan for my life and start living in relationship with the Divine architect of this plan?

Chapter Twenty

Letting the Past Die

IF WE ARE GOING TO LIVE IN THE SPACE OF FREEDOM, we have to let go of the past and choose to live right here, right now. We cannot be simultaneously living in the past and free of our egoic identity. The majority of our egoic identity is rooted in the past. The ego is mostly a collection of past memories, repetitive behaviors, and habits. Being free is the space of consciousness where we live unattached—beyond hope, fear, pain, and pleasure—and are living fully with all of our energy and presence in this moment. In order to live in this way, we cannot hold on to anything in our lives, especially the past. However, if we want to live in pain, we can choose to hold on to the past and grasp at our future. You see, the future never truly comes and we cannot change anything about the past, for it is now nonexistent. It is gone. The only time we have is this present moment, and in this moment is our freedom.

One day, I became upset with a good friend of mine because he was not living up to my expectations of him. Like a broken record, my mind continued reminding me over and over again about how he let me down. I was angry at this old friend—not for doing something new and unexpected, but for doing what he always does... he was essentially being himself. I had wanted him to be different, and as a result, I was suffering.

When I sat in meditation with these thoughts, and then took a few steps back from my own thinking, I realized that *I did not ask for these thoughts*; they simply arose within me, again and again. This insight was quite profound because I discovered that my thoughts were impersonal. They did not belong to me. They simply arose in an impersonal and repetitive fashion. Most of us incorrectly assume that our thoughts are *our* thoughts—that we create them and that they belong to us.

In a very impersonal way, our egoic nature brings thoughts into our consciousness, mostly in a predictable and repetitive fashion. Our ego creates a virtual reality within our minds by repeating the past over and over again. Yet this past is no longer present—whatever experience happened has come and gone and a new moment is here. But our mind continues to repeat the past, replaying it over and over again. Most of us become engaged and entranced by this movement of mind, often spending the majority of our lives living in this virtual reality of the past.

If we want to be free, we have to be willing to let our thoughts die in the openhearted spaciousness of our true nature. We have to be willing to not touch what we think. We must see our thoughts as impersonal movements of mind—and let them come and let them go, like the passing cars on a freeway. To do this, we must be willing to allow our attention to move to somewhere greater than the virtual reality presented in our minds.

We can bring our attention to the movement of our breath or to the sky which is always present and spacious. The sky is our constant reminder that there is alive, ever-present space all around us. This space is also within us. If we close our eyes, we see this empty space within. We can experience this spaciousness if we simply bring our attention to the space out of which all of our thoughts, emotions, feelings, and sensations arise. This may be a new practice for us, but if we want to begin to experience freedom, we must step into the space of freedom and begin to live from here.

Most of us are unwilling or too busy to slow down and experience this space. Instead, our unconscious and unquestioned minds lead the way. In a very unconscious way, our minds habitually look to our thought stream for a reference point for our identity, and as a result we suffer from this false identification. Our minds assume an identity based on our past thoughts. Whatever these thoughts tell us about ourselves, we unconsciously assume is us. If our thoughts tell us we are sad or angry or an alcoholic or worthy or unworthy, we believe this is what we are and define ourselves in this way. But what we are is much greater than our thoughts about ourselves.

To test this teaching experientially, we can bring our attention to the space out of which our thoughts arise. As we do this, we will discover a spaciousness which is our very essence. Our thoughts are simply passing phenomena; our essence is what is here all the time. This essence is waiting for us to come home, to let the constant stream of thoughts die, and to rediscover our Divinity which has been here in every moment of our life. We have been mistakenly taught by our collective humanity to think we are the movement of our minds and, unfortunately for us, these minds are quite insane. These minds are not the truth of us. The truth is that we are that which has been here silently in every moment. The question is, can we be so bold to discover this for ourselves? Can we drop into this silence right now and experience for ourselves if this is true?

Practice: If There Was No Memory of the Past

One night, my teacher Adyashanti asked, "If there was no memory [of the past], how can there be a self?" The self, our egoic nature, is created and sustained through our memory. If we have no memory of the past or gave up our identification with our past, what then would we be? This can be a liberating inquiry for us if we sit with it deeply.

What are we *really* if we gave up looking to our past to define us?

It is a funny question to ask. The ego has no idea what to do with such a question. But if we sit with it, we will see that no self can exist without memory. We certainly do not cease to exist if we let go of our relationship with memory. If we sit with this question and directly experience what is here, we may notice a spacious luminous Awareness is here in the present moment, whether we have a reference point of memory or not.

If you do not notice this, you can ask again, "What am I when I am not self-referencing to the past for my identity? What is here all the time, beyond my ideas and memories of the past, without my hopes for the future?"

If you put your attention fully on the *direct felt experience of this moment*, what do you notice is here?

Chapter Twenty-One

Gratitude

T HE FURTHER WE WALK ALONG THE PATH, the more thankful and gracious we become in our relationship with life. This feeling of gratitude arises when we choose to experience life through the vision of our heart which is naturally open, fully complete, and embracing of all of life. As we begin to live more and more in this new reality of our being, we will experience a deep appreciation for the Divine and an overwhelming intimacy with all of Life. This perspective is available to us all, no matter where we are on the path, because this space is our very nature. Unfortunately, this is not the perspective that most of us live in. Most of us live in a deeply divided judgmental reality where the mind is lost in confusion between hope and fear, unsure which way to go, with multiple voices offering opposing views, opinions, and arguments.

Some time ago, for about a decade, I struggled to make ends meet. I was a young, single father and could not pay the bills. I fell into enormous debt and every month had the fear of soon becoming homeless. Many of us know the experience of financial stress to one degree or another; when we are faced with financial stress, the first thing that happens is that our mind begins to spin very fast, trying to find some solution, while simultaneously emitting feelings of insecurity. In this state of mind, hopes and fears spin in all directions.

If we believe in this story generated by our mind and take our thoughts to be the truth of Reality, we will suffer greatly.

But, if we can slow down, take some deep breaths, and open our eyes to the vast perspective that is here, we will be able to step out of our suffering and see Reality.

As we open to each moment in this way, we realize that the world is wonderful and beautiful, just as it is. We see that we are not actually going to drown in life; we may still not be able to pay the bills, but this does not actually mean that we are in true danger. We may need to do something to take care of this situation, but the truth is we are not always in real danger like our fearful mind has been telling us. The relative reality may be that we do not have enough in this moment, but the greater Reality is that the world is wonderful, beautiful, and abundant whether we have millions of dollars in the bank or are in debt.

It makes sense to assume that our mind is more likely to be calm if we have our basic needs met, but ironically there seems to be great mental and emotional suffering regardless if we are rich or poor. This comes as quite a shock to most of us, but study after study shows there is no relationship between material wealth and happiness. Some studies even show that the poorest and most impoverished people are among the happiest. The root of suffering is not wealth or material goods or lack of them, it is our grasping and comparing mind. This universal suffering is caused by an unconscious belief in deficiency and lack. This mental and emotional belief in deficiency seems to always be running within us wherever we are at in life, whether we have great wealth, some wealth, or no wealth. But this program of deficiency is not the Truth of us. It is an aspect of our insecure egoic nature—biologically hardwired into us so that we continue working to have our basic needs met. However, this primal programming never recognizes that when we have our basic needs met it can stop producing the incessant stream of thoughts proclaiming deficiency. For most of us, this sense of deficiency continues whether we are rich or poor.

Our egoic nature is mostly a psychological force of insecurity and defensiveness which is programmed to be innately insecure so that it is always trying to protect us from harm. Our ego is always assessing lack and safety within us and our lives. This is helpful if we live with real scarcity or in a dangerous place, but not so helpful when we live in a safe environment with most of our basic needs met most of the time.

To discover the truth of what we are, we must be able to see and experience clearly what we are. One of the ways that we can begin to see and experience who we are is to come into the space of gratitude, because gratitude is a space outside of the nature of egoic insecurity and lack. When most people speak about gratitude, they are speaking about mentally being gracious through steering the mind toward the positive. While that is both an important and helpful practice, what I am sharing here is much greater than just mentally counting our blessings or being positive. There is a space or energy of gratitude which naturally arises through allowing our own Beauty to see itself in us and everything around us.

Gratitude is not really about counting our blessings; it is about seeing life through our hearts. It is about falling in love with life. It is about seeing beauty everywhere, even if our egoic nature is trying so hard to tell us otherwise. This requires that we step out of our egoic perspective and into the space of our heart—that we actively bring our awareness into the warm, alive presence of our being nature. As we see and experience ourselves in this way, we open to the space of unity, the space of true love. We see the world as us, and us as the world, as vibrant, alive, and Beautiful. And when we do, everything changes. We become happy to be alive, happy to be Life itself, and totally fulfilled by what we are—not by what we possess.

Many people have said to me, "I cannot do this. I cannot see beauty anywhere." This is true if we are trying to see out through the lens of our confused or suffering minds. But we all can stop for a minute, or two minutes, or an hour, and bring our awareness into our hearts, breathe into our hearts, and simply watch the leaves dance in the wind, the rain fall from the sky, and listen to the birds chirping. We can stop our busy lives, look into the eyes of our crying child and say, "Hello God, you are so beautiful, you are so perfect, I am so thankful to be here with you. How can I help you, dear one?"

Practice: Gratitude

1. Take the backward step out of egoic identification and come into the space of the heart.

2. Breathe, feel, and experience the quiet goodness and tender beauty of your heart.

3. Invite this inner radiance to wake up more fully and begin to spread throughout your being and overflow into your life.

4. See the world from this space of quiet joy.

5. Notice the vast immeasurable abundance of the sky, trees, mountains, rivers, oceans, and of life Itself.

6. Notice the beauty in small things... the sound of a bird, the eyes of your dog, a neighbor's face, and in each breath you take.

7. Open, open, open to this world—big and small, up and down, past and future, light and dark—what is happening now, all radiating with a subtle light of Divinity.

Practice: Where I Shut Down

We often shut down when we feel lack. This is the habitual response of ego. This practice can help you to find the places where you shut down within yourself.

1. What areas in your life do you feel struggle or lack? Such areas may be your finances, relationships, family, experiences of love, body image, physical health, job or career, spiritual practices, and your connection with God. Choose one area to work with for the rest of this practice.

2. Sit quietly and invite healing to come forth in whatever area your struggle or lack may be.

3. Take some more time and continue to invite even more love, healing, strength, courage, abundance, and intelligence to come forward into your feeling of struggle or lack.

4. Feel deeply *into your heart* (not your thinking mind) and ask the following questions. As you sit quietly, allow the intuitive guidance of your heart to arise.

    *   What do I need to change or do differently in this area of my life?

    *   What attitudes or habitual or negative beliefs are holding me back?

    *   Am I willing to change something that is not working and work toward change, despite a fear of failure?

    *   Am I willing to call forth the presence and power of God to come into my life and give me the strength to grow, change, and heal?

- Am I willing to acknowledge the paradox of absolute abundance and relative lack, and not fall into despair when I experience the relative lack in a difficult or prolonged way?

- Am I open and receptive to the Beauty and Intelligence of Life?

- Can I love and embrace all the places within that have felt ignored, abandoned, traumatized or lacking love in any way?

- Can I sit with these places and shower them with love and peace, until the healing within is total and complete?

- Can I commit to my own healing so that my heart can realize that what I am is Love Itself?

Chapter Twenty-Two

Pain: Possibly Our Greatest Teacher

MOST OF US SPEND A GREAT EXTENT OF OUR LIVES avoiding pain, but most of us do not spend any time examining what pain actually is. This is because we are all so frightened of feeling. This fear of feeling keeps us from discovering deep truths and beauty in our lives. The overwhelming tendency to avoid pain at all costs is wired into the biological fabric of our nervous system and psychological nature. Because of this wiring, we automatically and unconsciously assume that pain is bad and must be avoided. However, beyond our egoic relationship with pain is a greater understanding which comes from looking deeply at what pain is, and how we relate to it.

When we begin to mature on the spiritual path, we find that the majority of spiritual and psychological growth comes from *becoming intimate with pain*. When we first step on the path, we often think we grow from achieving this, that, and the other thing... and sometimes this is the case. But a much greater experience unfolds as we learn to open to every experience and allow it to be our teacher. As we do so, we discover the nondual nature of Life. We discover that nothing is outside of the Divine and that everything is here to open us whether it feels wonderful or terrible. We see, experientially, that all of Life is a movement of Divinity.

If we reflect deeply on our lives, we will see that, by far, our greatest growth comes from facing our pain and meeting it with love. Whether it was learning to love the places that scare us, or to grieve, forgive, let go, or to be kind and gentle to ourselves, all of this became available when we were willing to look at something uncomfortable—when we were willing to come into our hearts instead of habitually meeting life from our defended minds. When we come into our hearts, we naturally become willing to experience all of life as it is right here, right now. We become willing to experience even pain—because our heart is something much greater than our habitual egoic nature.

Our heart is not fleeting and timid like our mind. Our heart is the manifestation of the Divine in form. Our heart has no boundaries and no limitations. Our heart is the same heart of Christ or Buddha. Our heart is strong, powerful, wise, and compassionate, and it is *always* overflowing with love. There is no end to it.

The love, power, and presence of your heart is the very mysterious force animating your being right now. It is completely ineffable, far different than the conditioned nature of ego. When we are willing to step into our hearts, we become fearless and are willing to examine our lives from a place of freedom. This freedom, this Divinity, is naturally willing to meet and become intimate with pain, because the nature of the heart is to love all, even that from which our mind would run.

Any mother who sees a crying child naturally bends down and picks up the child. She does this without thought, without hesitation. She simply acts as a movement of love. This is the nature of the heart. Yet most of us do not value ourselves enough to do the same with our own pain. So we must learn how.

This comes when we are willing to stop avoiding our pain and instead sit with our pain and become close with it. It is in that moment when we will discover something quite remarkable; that pain is not what we think it is. It is not the story in our minds. It is not the story of our emotional hurt. Pain is something much more extraordinary. When we open to pain and become deeply intimate with it, we discover that pain is made up of the same substance which makes up everything in the universe—energy. We see that pain is repressed energy, stuck energy, or energy that we are channeling in the opposite direction of life. When we meet pain on the level of energy, we often find that this energy simply needs to move, untwist, and unwind. We see that this energy is pregnant with the potential of growth, transformation, and our very evolution.

In a practical sense, viewing pain simply as energy gives us the opportunity to see it for what it is, not something we need to run from. We can see pain as something to work with, something to listen to, and something to open up to. From this space, we can begin to see pain as a doorway, as our teacher coming to us in an unexpected form. As we fearlessly open in this way, we grow... we evolve into something greater than what we were before. We open to the nondual nature of Reality, and we discover that nothing is outside of or separate from God, even our experience of "pain."

This may sound philosophical, but it is not. For this work to become practical, we have to meet ourselves on the level where we are at. For example, in my own life, I can remember a time when I was in a heated argument with a friend of mine. We were working on a project at work together and I was very frustrated because what I wanted others to do on the project was not being done. My friend was the project leader and I continually brought my complaints and criticism to him with the hope that he would address it. He had a "hands off" work philosophy, so my concerns went unaddressed. I continued to voice my complaints to him until one day he exploded on me, calling me "negative" along with some other colorful adjectives. I became defensive and argued back. My emotions became loud and so did his.

At some point, I saw that we were getting nowhere. I recognized that I could not change him, so I dropped my argument. I breathed into my emotions. I felt the heat and energy of my emotions and his. I felt the energy of my anger and opened to it. As I did this, I felt the energy of power move through my body.

I realized that we were both angry about our unexpressed power in the group. We both were leaders, but we led differently. I could not have come to this realization until I let go of my argument, honored my emotions, and opened to the deeper energy at the heart of the anger. When I met my frustrations and painful emotions, I discovered that there was an aspect of my nature which was not being expressed in my life. This situation challenged me to find a healthy avenue for its expression. And so I took my "negative" complaining energy and channeled it in a positive way by connecting to the people who were enthusiastic and able to implement my ideas instead of complaining to someone who was uninterested. I saw that there was a part of myself who was being lazy and complaining instead of being proactive and taking charge. My complaining and anger became a doorway to let go of my argument of why I was right, allowing me to step into a spacious freedom, and to become more embodied and expressive of my innate power in this world.

The pain that arises within us, almost always, has some level of truth to teach us. When we meet this pain within ourselves at the level of energy, we are much more likely to discover the truth that it wishes to teach. If we meet ourselves on the level of mind, we will often stay stuck in our "mental story" and be confused by our own defensiveness. If we meet ourselves only on the level of our "emotional story," we will continue to stay wounded and hurt.

This experience of pain can become transformational when we are willing to let go of our defensiveness, feel the pain, and allow it to move, transform, or change on the level of energy. As it begins to move, we discover the truth of our pain and are able to learn from it fully. By doing this work, we open to a greater perception of life where we see that pain is not something bad and to be avoided, but something profound and extraordinary. As we open in this way, our whole experience of life changes from being based in ego and fear to being an expression of nondual freedom, which only becomes available as we fearlessly embrace pain and discover a Truth greater than how we feel.

Practice: Learning from Pain

- What experience of pain in my life am I avoiding?

- What can I learn from this experience? Am I viewing this experience in a defended way or an open and curious way?

- What Divine aspects of myself does this experience challenge me to step into? Will embracing this experience challenge me to be greater than who I am today? How must I grow in order to meet this experience with Love, compassion, strength, and equanimity?

- If I meet this situation from my heart, how will my experience be different than if I meet this experience from my ego?

Practice: Meditation on Pain

1. Sit and become quiet. Scan your body and feel all the aspects of your experience that you may be avoiding. Feel any anger, sadness, or other difficult sensations. Breathe deeply and fully here.

2. Notice the tendency to run or avoid these sensations, yet open to them. Feel the heat of anger or the tenderness of sadness. Openheartedly feel whatever is within. Notice that the experience intensifies temporarily, and then after some time softens.

3. If you find yourself lost in the story of the pain, simply come back to the sensations of the pain, and breathe.

4. Notice that these sensations do not kill you. Notice that what you are is greater than any sensation—that your awareness is greater than the pain.

5. From this space come into your heart and meet the sensations of pain with love. Allow the goodness of your heart to meet the pain. We do this by feeling the pain, breathing into the pain, accepting the pain, and loving the pain.

6. Now experience the pain simply on the level of energy—without any story attached to it. Feel the energy. Is it hot or cold? Tight or tense? Stuck or flowing? Feel the direct experience of this energy and breathe here for some time. Allow this energy to move, soften, untwist, and release.

Chapter Twenty-Three

Forgiveness

I F WE ARE GOING TO LIVE IN A HAPPY AND SANE WAY, we have to know how to work with our egoic minds. If our egoic minds are busy being lost in pain and confusion, we cannot be happy. This life here on Earth is a realm where we grow mostly through painful experiences and much of this pain cannot be avoided. No matter how hard we try, we will continually be faced with difficult, challenging, and painful circumstances; whether we are rich or poor or whether we are a criminal or a saint, this world will challenge us to evolve through continuously pushing our buttons. This is a fact of life.

Many of us in the spiritual world have an idea that if we become really enlightened one day, then we will no longer experience difficulty. But difficulty is part of the fabric of life. Difficulty is what makes us grow. We are all challenged—from the Dali Lama to the convict on death row—there is no escape from this truth. However, we can be skillful in how we relate to these challenges. One of the greatest teachings of both Jesus and the Buddha was forgiveness. Forgiveness is a skill that we can develop, it is an attitude we can possess. It is not distant from us, for it is the very nature of our hearts. To discover the power of forgiveness is to discover our own compassion, humility, power, and ultimately our freedom.

Most of us who have been harmed do not want to forgive. We hold on to our pain from the past as a reminder that we do not want that experience to repeat itself. We are afraid that if we let our guard down we will be hurt again. This act of holding on to pain is an egoic defense against further pain. But our ego does not understand that who and what we truly are, cannot be harmed. Our essence can never be truly harmed. Our bodies, our ego, our personality, and our humanity can be harmed and be deeply hurt, this is true—but our eternal nature outlives all experiences.

To the ego it is foolish to forgive; our egos do not understand why it is actually wise to forgive because our egos live in the perspective of fear and defensiveness. Forgiveness is a powerful act of love for our own selves. Forgiveness is a willingness to see that who we are is stronger than what we think or feel, and that what we are is greater than any pain and any act of violence. If we take a moment and truly reflect on all the pain of our lives, can we see that we have *outlived every experience*, no matter how painful? We outlived it all. One day we will even discover that we have outlived our very own death.

When we reflect on a painful memory, we may notice two experiences: (1) it was painful when it happened, and (2) if we continue to harbor anger or resentment about that experience, we continue to suffer in the present moment. When we reflect on our relationship to our experience, we see that we have the power to free ourselves from whatever the past was. This is a radically different orientation than that of being a victim of our experience. To be a victim is to live in the realm of blame, the realm of ego.

To live in the realm of freedom, we have to discover that we have the power in each and every moment to choose how we relate to the world. We do not have to deny what happened; we can honestly admit that the experience was painful, traumatic, or even brutal. We can also see that this experience did not destroy us. It may have hurt our ego, our body, or our sense of self, but ultimately, we see that who we are at the core of our being, remained unharmed.

Most of us do not like this teaching because it fully dismisses the story of our pain. The story of our pain is, by far, one of the most cherished identities of our egoic nature. As long as we have a painful story floating around in our consciousness, we will have a strong egoic identity. If we are going to be ruled by this egoic identity, we only have to hold on to our pain and keep this story alive. Yet if we are going to live in the world of freedom, we must discover our own power. We must be willing to take full responsibility for our lives, our pain, and our relationship to it. A great power can come to us through the act of letting go and forgiveness. Most of us, though, are unable to simply rise above and choose to live in our eternal nature in every moment; therefore, we must learn about forgiveness and our true power by allowing our heart to be broken open by the painful experiences of life. We must start where we are, even if that means we start while in the depths of pain and egoic confusion.

The Buddha once said that being angry is like holding a hot coal in your hand and not letting it drop. Forgiveness is the act of letting go for the sake of freedom—for the sake of our own happiness and sanity. This does not mean that we approve of the action we are forgiving nor that we think the action was right. We forgive because we do not want to carry poison in our minds and hearts. If there is an injustice which occurs in our lives and we can do something about it, we take the necessary actions—this is wise. Maybe we need to leave the situation, set a clear boundary, or call the police. But ultimately, if we want to be happy and live in our true nature—which is open, free, and undefended—we must let go of the past... we must let go of the injustice, and come into our own present moment freedom.

In order to let go of the past, we may need to first take care of our emotional pain. If we are having trouble forgiving someone or something, it is because there is some aspect of ourselves which is feeling hurt or scared by whatever happened. Before we forgive, we must take care of our own pain; we must embrace that place within us which is hurting, meet it with love, and actually let this place within us know that we will not allow this injustice to harm us again. Our ego will not let go unless it knows that we are safe and free from harm. To help become ready to let go, we may first need to give ourselves full permission to be angry or sad about the event, and then meet this pain with a motherly love—a love which listens to our own pain and compassionately meets ourselves with understanding. We may need some time to allow this pain to come forward again and again while we meet it from the love and compassion of our own heart. This unfolding may take a day, a week, a month, or a year. The more fully we meet ourselves with love and compassion, the quicker this process will go.

After we have met our emotional world with compassion and love, we then forgive as an act of letting go of the pain and letting go of the story in which the pain happened. As we do so, we are saying, "Yes that was painful, and now it is done. I do not want to carry this pain or this anger any longer. I am consciously choosing to let this go. I am consciously choosing to forgive and to move beyond what once happened. I am choosing to see that whoever did this to me, was acting from a place of ignorance and pain. I see that the only way they could have done this is because they were not seeing clearly. I forgive them for being a human, who was scared or ignorant, just like me. I let go of this because I see that as I keep holding on to it, I continue to suffer. Now I am ready to be my normal happy self again. I forgive them and I stand in my own radiant Truth—happy, powerful, and free."

Practice: Inquiring to Forgive

- What sits heavy on my heart? Have I forgiven this person? Am I ready to forgive? What am I holding onto that is holding me back from letting go?

- What emotional pain do I need to embrace and meet with love first before I can forgive? Am I willing to take the time to do this work? Am I willing to feel this pain and meet it with my compassionate presence until it heals?

- What story can I let go of so that I can release this pain and move on? Does this story of injustice provide me with a sense of identity? Am I willing to live in a place beyond the story of how I have been wronged? What new story would I have to embrace or create in order to make this transition?

- Am I willing to stand in my power and choose to not be a victim of my past circumstances? Am I willing to be so bold as to take full responsibility for my life by choosing consciously how I relate to every experience which is given to me?

- Can I see that all beings make mistakes, just like me? Do I know that the only time people are mean is when they are scared, confused, or acting from ignorance? Can I see that the person who hurt me was scared, confused, or acting from ignorance?

- Am I ready to let go of this poison for my own sake?

Forgiveness is a radical act of Love.

A friend of mine once sent me this question on forgiveness: "A question that keeps coming up for me is, what is forgiveness, really? Is it to stop thinking about it? Or is it to stop feeling hurt and angry about it? Or is it to see that the one who hurt you just didn't know better? Or is it something else? What does forgiveness actually mean, in a down-to-earth practical way?"

Forgiveness is a radical act of Love. It is choosing to let go of the past for our sake—for our sanity. It is choosing to unplug from the past and to live fully in the present moment. It is choosing to reclaim our power and stand in our inherent Divinity. It is choosing to see that who and what we truly are cannot be harmed or hurt. It is consciously choosing to see life through the lens of our heart, not through the lens of our defended and wounded egoic nature.

The act of forgiveness can be invoked in many ways: we may simply decide to let go of whatever past experience we had that we did not like and come into the present. Or we might choose to tell the person who hurt us that, "I am not happy about what happened but it is okay, I understand and I forgive you," and simply move on. We may consciously choose to see life through the compassion of our hearts and simply admit that we are all human, and understand that when we do something less than Divine, it is because we were confused by our collective egoic nature.

Sometimes, though, forgiveness does not come so easy to us. We may first have to give ourselves permission to actually feel our pain and anger or our sadness and grieve fully before we are able to let it go. We do this by admitting we are human; we give ourselves permission to be totally honest and admit that we are struggling here in our humanity. We may have to take the time to feel our pain fully—all the levels and layers of it—and allow it to naturally release from our being before we can forgive someone or ourselves. We may have to look honestly at ourselves and admit our part. We may have to realize that the angry voices inside us are driving us crazy and we can no longer believe what we think about the situation, but admit and experience the sadness that these angry voices are shielding us from. We may have to admit that we are the ones creating our own pain, and then forgive ourselves for being deluded, for being confused, or for holding on to something which is killing us. There are countless ways we can come to the radical letting go of forgiveness.

Ultimately, forgiveness is about coming into our hearts and choosing to Love, to accept, to let go, to be free, to see clearly, and to come into the present moment and live our lives fully and powerfully. It is the choice to have all of our Being—all of our energy and power—in the present moment and not tangled up in the past. It is the radical choice to be here fully, now, and to be courageously open to what is.

The good news is that living in this way is not a choice. Life will relentlessly continue to challenge us and will actually force us to come into the present moment by making it too painful for us to hold on to the past. Life will force us to let go, because letting go is a natural aspect of life. We are actually wired to let go and be present. When we are present, we naturally feel wonderful, we feel alive, and we experience our own Divinity. When we are lost in the past, we feel terrible and this pain which we have held onto will one day become too unbearable for us, and so we will ask for another way. This way is the path of forgiveness.

Practice: Forgiveness

1. What is life asking you to let go of right now?

2. Are you willing to step into a new relationship with this past pain?

3. Can you open to the joy of letting go and the great freedom which comes with it?

~ Chapter Twenty-Four ~

Everything Comes and Goes—Be With What Remains

ONE OF THE MOST AMAZING TEACHINGS I RECEIVED from my teacher, Adyashanti, came in an unexpected way. I was driving across the San Luis Valley in Colorado, one of my favorite places in the world. It is a vast expansive valley that looks as if it should be on the cover of some new age book. At this point in my life, I was recently divorced, on the verge of bankruptcy, overwhelmed emotionally, grieving to no end, and trying to finish graduate school while raising two children. As I drove across the valley, all of this pain that I had been carrying erupted in tears and a huge surge of emotion. Under the pressure of it all, my emotional egoic mind cracked wide open as I drove at 70 mph into the valley. I felt my consciousness expand as big as the sky and simultaneously my emotional walls and defenses began to unravel in a seemingly endless letting go of tears and pain. Simultaneously, I was flooded with grief and expansive bliss in a way that was uncontainable in this small frame of mine. As my conscious spread and became one with the vast expanse valley, I smiled and let go into unimaginable freedom. This incredible satori flooded my being and seemed to change the fabric of what I knew myself to be.

When I went to my teacher and told him about my "awakening experience," I then asked him how I could continue to have this experience forever. Patiently, he told me, "Experiences come and go." And then he asked me, "What is it that is here in every moment?" His question hit me like a freight train. I stopped my unconscious outward grasping and seeking and I directed my attention to the present moment. I replied, "There is a quiet here, a still Silence and a vastness." He replied, "Good, just be with that." That was the end of our discussion. He did not care about my big experience of this or that. He did not care about my grasping or seeking or the current drama in my life. He simply reminded me to bring my attention to what is here in every moment. This question, though quite simple, changed my life forever.

If we want to know a true freedom, a freedom beyond all of our wonderful spiritual experiences, beyond our painful drama, and beyond our mental chatter, we must discover this truth that is not only here in every moment, but is the very fabric of our being. It is not that our spiritual experiences do not have value or are insignificant, they are. It is just that if we truly want to be free, we must discover a truth that is greater than all our experiences. We must discover a truth greater than the comings and goings of our minds. If we are deeply honest, we can find this truth right here, right now. If we directly experience this moment—not through the lens of our conditioned ego, but simply through our direct experience—we may ask ourselves, *what do I find?* In this moment, do I notice a silence—a silence so deep and inclusive that all sound arises out of this silence? Can I notice where my thoughts come from and dissolve into? Do I see the space where all experiences arise in? Is this space separate from the one who is observing it?

If we are going to directly experience freedom, we must directly experience the space of freedom as our own selves. Anything less is just philosophy. As long as we do not know *that which is here in every moment as the very fabric of our being*, we will be living in separation and delusion. When we do not know who we are, we easily mistake the arising of thoughts and feelings as what we are. When we make this error we live in suffering—simply because we believe that which is false, empty, and insecure to be our self. When we make this mistake, we experience unimaginable pain and confusion. But to know ourselves as the very space of freedom is to find never-ending lasting contentment.

Practice: Contemplate What Remains

1. Notice what is here in every moment, beyond thoughts and feelings. Notice what is here right now.

2. Deeply contemplate this question: "Can I separate myself from what is here in every moment?"

3. When you give yourself permission to be this experience beyond your mind, how do you feel? What do you know yourself to be? How do you relate to life?

4. Whenever you are swept away by your mind, you can again ask yourself, "What is here in every moment? Can I be so humble to live from this space?"

Chapter Twenty-Five

True Humility

It is through true humility that we discover our Divinity.

WHILE WRITING THIS BOOK, A FRIEND CAME BY and asked how I reconciled being humble and knowing myself as Divine. It was a wonderful question and something that I struggled with for many years. I had been trained for many years in a traditional Eastern spirituality which basically taught that the way to spiritual freedom was through denying my ego or personal sense of self. These ascetic beliefs were reinforced in me through reading countless books about the lives of Indian sages and Christian mystics. Even as a young child, I deeply resonated with the vows of poverty and often had past life memories of being a monk in many different traditions. It was crystal clear in my unconsciousness that I was unworthy, I did not belong here in this world, and the road to enlightenment is paved with poverty and lack. I continued to reinforce these beliefs with ascetic practices: I slept on the floor, meditated for hours each day, denied myself enough food to eat, spent all my time and energy focused on transcendence, denied myself supportive relationships, and always put myself last. Somehow, I assumed that these activities would lead me to an egoless freedom.

The problem with these types of teachings is that they may not lead us to enlightenment; ironically, they may lead us to feeling more unworthy and unhappy, which is one of the favorite dances of the ego.

Our ego actually becomes reinforced through feeling and being unworthy. It does so because the more we believe in an emotional identity in whatever form (worthy or unworthy), the more material the ego has to use to build its identity out of. Usually in life, we fall into believing either "I'm better than everyone" or "I'm unworthy of being here." Both beliefs are delusions. Many spiritual seekers fall into the "I'm unworthy" category because it is more spiritually acceptable, yet it is still a total delusion.

If we look at this dance of mind directly, how could we be unworthy of our Divinity? It is completely absurd. Our Divinity is the mysterious luminous force animating our being, entirely present in all moments. How could we not be worthy of what we are? We all are Divine; to deny this in ourselves is to deny the Divinity of one individual. For some reason, many of us can acknowledge the Divinity of others, but cannot include ourselves in this recognition. This is a form of spiritual violence. Denying our Divinity actually reinforces our egoic separation from our Divinity and supports us in continuing to live in our egoic reality. It is not an act of humility to deny ourselves the acknowledgment of what we are. We are an equal manifestation of the Divine in a human body, as is everyone else. The trouble begins when we think we are better than or more important than someone else. But when we wake up to the truth of what we are, we see that everyone and everything is Divine in their essence. We see that there can be no truth to the belief that we are more or less than anyone, unless we are seeing from the perspective of our ego, which, in its nature, constantly compares itself to others. The Truth is that we are all made of and are animated by the same one Divinity, and this Divinity radiates from everyone and everything in the Universe. We are, in fact, One essence. To know ourselves as God is an act of total humility. It asks us to see beyond our egoic conditioning and to see the Beauty of who and what we are. And as we do, we see the overwhelming Divinity of all.

Many individuals become confused as they hear this teaching for the first time. They sometimes ask, "How could this be that a criminal and myself are equally Divine?" A practical discernment shows us that different individuals manifest their Divinity differently. We tend to culturally honor those whose actions are "pure" or in alignment with our definition of good and spiritual. Everyone—from a criminal to a banker to the Buddha—is, in their essence, the One Divinity that pervades this universe. From an egoic perspective, it makes sense to honor one and not the other. The ego's function is to compare and contrast and divide Oneness into separate and manageable parts. From a place of Divine vision, however, it makes no sense to deny anyone or anything of their inherent luminous Divinity. We were created by the Divine to experience ourselves as Divine, not to experience ourselves as less or more. The very act of making ourselves less or more than others is to sin—to miss the mark.

The act of loving ourselves and honoring our Divinity and our expression on earth is an act of courageous love. We really do not need any more individuals practicing false humility and denying their Divinity in this world. What we need are individuals to stand in their truth and to actively live this truth if the world is going to evolve. We cannot fully love others if we do not love ourselves totally. The very act of loving ourselves allows our heart to come forward in its fullness and gives it permission to shine out to the world. As we do, so we become one with our Divinity in our inner and outer manifestation. It takes an amazing degree of humility to know oneself as the radiance of the universe. And as we become this radiant and humble, we see ourselves everywhere.

Ironically, our egos can create a whole identity and countless stories around the dance of not being good enough or being the best, all of which is pure delusion and leads to more egoic identification. Freedom comes from love and inclusion, not from exclusion and division. Nothing makes God happier than when we wake to the truth of ourselves, because then God gets an opportunity to again bask in the Light of Her Divinity in the form of You. What a gift we become to ourselves and our world when we are willing to see, embody, and express our Divinity in our human form. This courageous act of loving ourselves will forever change our world.

It can take us ages to let go of the many ways we limit ourselves by not honoring and believing in ourselves. From one perspective, it keeps us safe from really being open and vulnerable. As long as we live in unworthiness, we can hide behind our beliefs and not allow the world to reject us because we have already done the rejecting. It is a really painful dance to live in this way. This dance often begins when we are young because many of us were taught that we do not deserve to be here by parents who were too busy or who were unskillful in parenting or who were deeply suffering themselves. For many of us, our egos crystallized around an experience of rejection, and from this experience our egos then fabricated the story that we do not belong here. This story can continue within us for an entire lifetime if we fail to consciously question it.

Fortunately, for most of us, life becomes too painful to remain deluded for our entire lifetime. But many of us do spend decades of our lives believing the thought that somehow we do not belong. In my own life, I projected this belief in so many directions that it showed up everywhere: my relationships, jobs, finances, classes... and the world reflected this belief back to me in such a painful and miserable way that finally I went to one of my teachers and began to consciously work with my belief in my own unworthiness. My teachers challenged me to let go of these silly belief systems that allowed me to continue denying the goodness of myself. Paradoxically, and in a humble way, as I investigated these faulty belief systems, loved them, and allowed them to release, I discovered the hugeness and power of my Divinity. And I am humbled by it to this day. Happily, I continue to see this love and Beauty reflected back to me in the countless eyes of others.

Practice: Honest Inquiry

Sit quietly and deeply contemplate these questions:

- Do I believe that I am better or worse than others?

- Where did my ego crystallize when I was young? Did I have certain experiences which reinforced my beliefs?

- Am I willing to let go of my past conditioned identity and discover a new identity in the radiance of my own nature?

- Am I willing to meet these painful places within myself with love and humility?

Practice: Experiencing Radiance

1. Can you spend a few minutes staring in the mirror, looking directly into your own eyes? Can you see and experience your own radiance and light coming out of your eyes?

2. Does this practice make you smile, or do you become angry and resist your own beauty, perhaps because someone else told you otherwise? Can you meet any resistance that arises with love and compassion?

3. Can you look into the eyes of your partner, children, parents, or your pet and experience their radiance? Can you allow their

radiance to awaken your own radiance? Can you notice this radiance all around you: in the trees, the sky, the traffic, and even in the trash?

4. When you look from this openhearted clarity, how do you feel? When you meet life from this openness, do you notice the great unity and non-division of Life?

Practice: What Is Here Before Thought?

1. Sit quietly and directly experience what is here before, during, and after a thought arises. Feel and experience yourself beyond the mind, emotions, and beyond any psychological defenses.

2. If you become identified with a thought, emotion, or defensiveness, simply come back to the direct experience of you, which is prior to all of this.

3. As deeply as possible, experience your own self as that which is here in every moment, before thought.

The basic confusion...

At our core we are Divine. This is an indisputable fact. At our core is a fundamental mysterious aliveness. No one can deeply look into a baby's eyes and honestly admit that they do not see an incredible mysterious presence. No one can truly deny that we are alive, awake, and aware; but most of us never spend any time even wondering what this aliveness is or what this awareness is. We do not because we are completely identified with our egoic nature, the movement of our minds, and the trance of our current drama. As a result of this trance, we miss the direct experience of this divinity which we are. The onset of this trance first came about as we developed from being a baby to a toddler, when our egoic nature began to first arise in our consciousness between the ages of one and two. The purpose of our egoic nature is so that we can grow and develop as an individual form. In a sense, for God to know herself as another, She has to incarnate into form and develop some form of individuality. The ego is a necessary step in this development. The ego is not something bad that we need to go to war with or fight against. The ego is a tool of creation which helps creation to individuate itself, so that Creation can have the experience of Itself in the form of you.

As we (who are incarnations of the Divine) incarnate into this realm, we are incarnating into a world with laws, physics, and a collective consciousness. As our awake, alive essence incarnates into this world, it is perfect and completely Divine, for aliveness itself is God. The mysterious life which animates a tree, the ocean, the stars, and your very own being is Divine. No scientist will ever be able to figure out what this mysterious presence called life is. This presence, when it incarnates, is perfect, for it is God. As it comes into this world of evolution, this presence is given an egoic nature, a nature which is narrow, limited, and self-centered in comparison to Life Itself. This ego, though, has a purpose; it gives this incarnating Divinity (whose nature is complete undifferentiated oneness) the opportunity to individuate. A tree does not have an ego; a tree is the presence of God in matter. But this tree does not have the experience of being an individual who can move about, climb mountains, and fall in love. An ego helps us to individuate from God and know ourselves as you and I; it helps us to organize reality so that we can function in the world of form. An ego helps us to separate ourselves from our mother, and then from all of life, so that we can one day again discover ourselves as God. Our lives, our spiritual path is like a great disappearing and reappearing act.

When we first incarnate, before our ego has arisen within our consciousness, we live in the direct experience of oneness. My baby Ani, right now, has no idea that she is separate from her mom. When she plays with a toy, she is startled when she brings it to her face and the toy touches her head. She is startled because she had no idea that she was separate from the toy. She had no idea that there was a self, a body to run into. She lives in oneness. As she gets older, an ego will slowly begin to develop within her and be conditioned by her environment. At first, a very primitive ego arises within us which has the basic program to seek pleasure and avoid pain. This very primitive drive impacts our decisions for the rest of our lives. Many other basic survival programs also arise that help us to function in this world in a safe way. In addition, we are given countless egoic qualities from our families, the environment, and the collective consciousness of our human species which also color and veil this Divine presence which we are.

As a parent, we can watch the growth and development of this egoic nature. My baby is showered each day with love from her mother. All day long she is held and told how beautiful she is. Everywhere we go, people stop us and say, "That is a beautiful baby!" Through this experience of conditioning, she will know herself as beautiful, loved, and supported in the world. These experiences of positive conditioning will allow for her healthy egoic conditioning, as well as simply be reflections of what she already is in her Divine nature and presence.

Conversely, for example, if I taught my baby that her needs were not important, that she needs to be quiet all the time, and that she is not beautiful, her egoic nature would be conditioned by the ideas that she is not welcome here, not loved, and not divine. This type of conditioning leads one away from the truth of our nature—from the truth of our Divine essence. When we experience this type of conditioning, our ego begins to crystallize around the belief that we are not safe, and as a result, our ego grows and becomes more defensive and insecure. The more this type of conditioning is reinforced, the more the ego solidifies in defensiveness and insecurity. Even if our parents are "perfect," our ego, by its very nature, will arise and solidify around some form of egoic identity.

However, this egoic identity is inherently insecure because there is no solid stable "self" at the core of the ego. This was what the Buddha was speaking about when he said there is no solid stable self. He meant that when we deeply examine our egoic nature, we never find any "self" which is solid and permanent. Therefore, why defend it, why uphold it, why become upset? When we defend our ego, we are essentially defending an illusion. The ego is basically an arising psychological phenomenon that we unconsciously identify with. This identity was given to us by nature and by our conditioning; it is not who we inherently are. Our presence—which is prior to ego—is who we are. Our fundamental confusion is that we have identified with our ego—our conditioning—as who we are. Meanwhile, we have missed the quiet and alive beautiful presence that is reading this sentence right now. To know ourselves as this presence, we must unhook from our minds and live in the direct experience of this mystery which we are. We must be willing to stand in the space that is before thought, before ego, and before conditioning. We must be willing to experience that which is here in every moment. As we step into this world of what we truly are, we open the door to life beyond ego, beyond thought, beyond judgment, and beyond walls. We step into the realm of our True Nature, which is completely Ineffable.

Chapter Twenty-Six

The Impersonal Nature of Mind

IF WE STOP AND REFLECT UPON OUR OWN MINDS, what we find is a collection of past thoughts and experiences, most of which was given to us by life. Our education, our beliefs, our politics, our cultural norms, and even our neurotic behavior was given to us in one form or another. It can be life changing simply to take the time and examine where all of the contents of our minds come from, and quite humbling to discover that almost every thought, belief, and even emotional response was given to us by life. When we discover this, we see how *impersonal* our personal lives are.

When we come into this world, our minds are empty and free. And as we grow, we absorb all of the thoughts and beliefs of our environment. We absorb what our parents teach us about life, what our education teaches us about life, and what our friends and partners tell us about ourselves. We accept the thinking of the cultural norms, and then these thoughts become our thoughts. This collection of "our thoughts" then becomes our identity. It is rare for any of us to actually have an original thought, although most of us unconsciously assume that everything we think is our own creation.

For those of us who are deeply identified with our thinking minds, we may resist this reality and argue, "If I am not my thoughts then what am I?" This resistance arises because, perhaps for the first time in our life, our egoic nature is being seen for what it is... an impersonal mask. This discovery can be quite shocking to our sense of self—that our thoughts and identity are impersonal and have nothing really to do with us. When we actually see that our thoughts do not belong to us, we may then begin to wonder, "What am I, really?"

As we begin to investigate this question, a new world opens within us... a world where we are not unconsciously identified with our conditioned thoughts. We may ask ourselves, "Is this thought me? Is this emotion me? Is this feeling me?" If a thought, emotion, or feeling is truly what we are, it would have to be present with us in every single moment of our lives. However, most of our thoughts, feelings, and emotions have a very short lifespan, sometimes only a few seconds. What we truly are has been with us our entire life, in every moment.

Practice: The Impersonal Nature of Thought

To begin to see the impersonal nature of your thoughts, ask yourself the following questions:

- Where did this thought come from? When did I first begin believing this thought?

- What cultural norms have I accepted as Reality?

- What familiar beliefs do I allow to define me and go unexamined?

- What are my beliefs about relationships? Where did these beliefs come from?

When we begin to question our thoughts and beliefs in this way, we may find that our thoughts and beliefs about relationships came from our parents' marriage or from Hollywood movies and TV shows. We may find that our culture has taught us that it is okay to have ongoing wars as long as we do not see any dead and wounded bodies on the evening news. We may notice that our political beliefs are simply a rebellious response to our parents and that we do not really know what we actually believe. When we begin to question ourselves in this way, we cut through the personal nature of our impersonal identity. And so we ask ourselves, "Who am I before I was born into this family?"

Chapter Twenty-Seven

Self or No Self?

"**W**HY DO SOME TEACHERS SAY THAT THERE IS NO SELF, but in my experience I have a self?" I am often asked this question in one form or another and find that most individuals on the path have no real idea how the teachings on "no self" are relevant to our everyday lives. In the past, this teaching was reserved for monks and nuns who were living ascetic lives in the monastery. As the wisdom traditions have spread to the outside world, many are now wondering what these teachings are about and if they have any significance to lay people and householders.

The "self" has traditionally been referred to as all the psychological forces, memories, thoughts, beliefs, hopes, fears, judgments, dreams, desires, and conditioning that make up our ego. Basically, the self is everything that most individuals refer to as "me." From a spiritual perspective, all these things that we normally call "me" are simply psychological forces that pass through the space of what we truly are— vibrant and alive spacious awareness. To get a glimpse of what life is like if we saw through the illusionary nature of the self, we would have to let go of all of that we normally refer to as ourselves, surrender who we think we are, and step into the great spacious unknown.

To truly live this, beyond just having a momentary glimpse, we have to be fully taken by the Divine. It is Grace that comes and takes us, usually when we are far, far along the path. What begins to happen is that various parts of our egoic identity literally drop away from us and we find our actual identity in the Spacious wonder that we are.

This may seem like some profound spiritual state, but it is the state we are all born into. When a baby comes into this world, it is free and has no identity, it has no ego. Of course, at some point, through both nature and nurture, we develop an ego. This is healthy and part of our development as individuals. But because life does not always go easy for us, we experience pain, suffering, and growth. As a result of this growth process, our ego splits into healthy and unhealthy shadow aspects. And for many of us, the unhealthy shadow aspects of our ego tend to dominate our way of being and interacting with the world.

However, at some point after we have matured on the path, when we have seen through and taken the time to heal these neurotic aspects of self, they begin to heal and dissolve and are no longer present within us. At first, it may seem as if "we" are doing the healing and dissolving of our egoic tendencies, but ultimately it happens through the process of Grace. It would be arrogant to assume that we can let go of our egoic nature from within the space of our ego. This process of letting go of egoic aspects of the self happens through a mysterious act of Grace. It does not happen through the will of our ego or by means of our spiritual disciplines. It happens through a total impersonal surrender. This process may happen with a quiet and simple falling away of our anger or neurotic tendencies, or it may come through a huge dramatic experience of letting go. We may quietly notice that some aspect of our reactionary self no longer arises, or that perhaps a huge aspect of our egoic mind fell away after surrendering in a deep and profound way, leaving us feeling completely disoriented.

It can happen that when someone close to us dies, such as our spouse or child, we are left empty, awestruck, and disoriented because we no longer are a "husband" or "wife" or "mother" or "father." A huge aspect of our identity has been taken away by life. We may wake up in the morning not knowing who we are without our loved one and the

157

assumed identity that went along with them. We may realize that we are no longer a "husband" or "wife" or "mother" or "father" and yet, paradoxically, we may now feel empty and free of this former identity. It can also happen that one day we find that we are no longer interested in any of the thoughts in our mind or in our spiritual identity (e.g., being a Buddhist or a Christian, etc.) and we are left open, empty, and free. We may find that all at once, we lose the ability to judge, argue, and complain about our "old story" and notice that our whole orientation to life has changed in a surprising or shocking way. Sometimes we are left spellbound and are not even sure how to respond to life because in the past we were so full of the judging and complaining thoughts and now that those aspects of our mind have fallen away, we really do not have anything to say. When these changes happen quickly, they can be quite disorienting. If a large aspect of our self is constantly judging others and we have many friends who join us in this judging and gossiping tendency, we may go through an identity crisis when we wake up out of this neurotic tendency and can no longer relate to those same friends or our life in the same judging and gossiping way.

But what is more common or likely is that over a number of years, we find that various aspects of our egoic selves have slowly become nonexistent. This is what the Buddha was speaking about when he spoke of the illusion of a solid personal self. He was reminding us that all of these thoughts which arise in our minds that we identify with are temporary and empty of any inherent solidity; therefore, they cannot be who and what we are. When we truly examine this, it is quite profound to discover that who we thought we were was simply an impermanent movement of impersonal mental and emotional phenomena. When we lose this identification with our minds, we lose who we thought we were and we discover ourselves to be the very space in which this impermanent mind arises. When we discover ourselves to be this space, we experience the oneness of space, the inclusive nature of space, the freedom of space, the emptiness of space, and the aliveness of space. It is a radical change from the limited nature of our egoic minds.

As this radical reorientation deepens, much of our egoic personality no longer arises within our consciousness. The falling away of the false self is nothing anyone could ever really want because it is so unimaginable; even talking about it is difficult because where it comes from is so far outside the realm of the collective consciousness. This process is the extinction of much of what we thought ourselves to be, especially our will, our sense of self-importance, our hopes, dreams, aversions, and our judgments about life. No ego—even the spiritual ego—could ever want its own dissolution. But at some point after a deep and profound awakening, much of our egoic nature begins to fall away. Not because we want it to, but because these egoic aspects are taken from us by something Greater. In their place, we are left with unimaginable quiet and vibrant spaciousness.

Some of us have experienced wonderful moments when our sense of self drops away in deep meditation or at the end of a long retreat. Usually this is a temporary experience and the egoic self reappears, sometimes only a few moments later. There are yogis in this world who live from this space of having little to no self. Some of them live in caves and have disciples who feed and take care of their bodily needs. The very presence of these yogis may do something very wonderful for the consciousness of the planet. For most of us, though, this will not be our own life experience. To those of us living in the Western world, living in a cave as a sage or swami with no self is not very practical, desirable, or even attainable. However, this process of dissolving identity can look very practical and manifest powerfully in our lives if we are willing to get out of the way and deeply surrender from beyond ourselves.

If we look at the definition of ego—our habits and desires and conditioning and our sense of "me-ness"—the act of letting go of much of this would make us available to be moved by something much deeper than our personal wants and needs or agendas. When we become parents, for example, we naturally get a taste of being selfless; we give our lives to our children. For the first time in our life, we naturally put someone else's needs before our own. My wife lives in this way, putting our daughter's needs before her needs. She is up all night taking care of her baby, changing her diapers and breastfeeding her. As a parent she is living beyond ego, selflessly.

It is important to make a distinction between being selfless and having no self. Being selfless is when we put others first. Most of us have met individuals who act selflessly and are always putting others first. This can come from the goodness of our hearts, as in the case of my wife, or it can come in a different way which actually creates more ego. There can be an egoic identity built out of this selfless behavior; we get to be the martyr, or we get to be the hero, or we get to be loved as a result of our kind actions. But to live from the space of no self is not simply about putting others before ourselves; having no self means we are empty of self-absorption or concern. The only way we really notice this no self is in the *absence of self*. We may notice that there is very little within us for life to rub against. We may no longer have a political view to maintain or argue. We may not care anymore if people are disappointed in us. We may no longer look to our parents or our partners in a needy way for love. We only notice that we do not care much about the things that we cared so much about in the past. We notice the disappearance of these egoic wants, needs, and drives. Or, put differently, these egoic wants, needs and drives do not arise within us anymore. Imagine that the egoic need of looking to our parents or our partners to love us a certain way so that we can feel and experience loved—dissolves. Instead we feel absolutely complete, free, empty, and that we could care less about them loving us a certain way or ever being different than they are. In the space of no self, this neediness dissolves and we are left with the quiet presence of Love as our very nature.

To get a sense of what this space would be like in regard to our anger or the need to be right, we may imagine the most sticky, personal dramatic mess that could arise in our lives and how we may have responded from our egoic nature in the past. Now imagine that this same situation comes forward in our life and nothing moves inside us. Imagine that someone who we deeply care about screams, "I hate you!" and there is no one within us to get hurt or to be angry or to argue. We do not even put up our psychological walls or defenses because there is nothing here to defend. This is what it is like to live from the space of no self. This "no one" is not some cold dead robotic being but is instead the space of compassion. Instead of our identity being made up of our wants, needs, desires and agendas, we are living from the hugeness of Silence, and now this Silence acts through us as Us.

It is important to note that some sense of self, which is unique to us, does remain. It is not that every aspect of our personality and egoic nature is forever dissolved; the Dali Lama has a personality that is different from the personality of That Nich Hanh, and yet both these beings live from this space. What is different about them is that their personalities are more fluid and flexible and they rest in the deepest Peace as their being, instead of being trapped in the trance of egoic identity.

Many individuals are afraid of this space of peace because they fear that they will no longer exist. While it is true that in this space much of our neurotic egoic nature will dissolve, there remains a functioning healthy personality. Most of us do not have to worry that we will turn into a completely empty vessel. As long as we are in form, we will have some degree of egoic nature, and this nature will be growing and evolving. The less egoic nature we have, though, the easier it is for this Silence to move through us, as Us. It is difficult for this Silence to be transmitted through us if we are busy arguing with our boss or mother-in-law.

If we want to begin to head in the direction of this realm of unimaginable freedom, two things are required: total surrender and total cooperation with Grace. Imagine what our lives would be like to live this deeply unified with God.

I can remember the first time I experienced the falling away of self. A good friend of mine came to me, very angry with an intense argument. In a moment of Grace, my entire sense of self just dropped away. I had nothing to defend, no point of view to argue, no walls or defenses up, and his anger was experienced as a very powerful energy that was neither good nor bad, but simply loud. There was space for him to continue on with his angry perspective and space for my ego to be nonexistent. It was difficult for me to even comment on or make a judgment about what was going on or what had happened, for my mind had fallen away. It may even sound crazy to say that there was instead a tremendous Love, but not a love coming from me that I was creating or bestowing upon him or the situation—it seemed as if everything that was arising was happening in the container of Love. There was no past, no wounds, no expectations, no desires; instead, there was an overwhelming Unity with Life Itself.

This process of dissolving is not something that I could ever have imagined or even desired because it is so absent of anything. When it comes, it does so like a thief in the night, leaving us spaciously disoriented without a past to refer to. It takes not what we think we want to get rid of, but what it wants from our egoic way of being; it is the most impersonal process. Often, we do not even know it has happened until we reflect and remember, "Oh, I used to get so livid in that situation, and now I do not even care." The most shocking aspect of the dissolving of self is that it is so quiet inside, as if the silence of the entire universe is here in this moment, even in the midst of a so-called painful experience.

Despite this falling away of the egoic aspects of self—because we are human and our egoic nature tends to be extensive—we may find ourselves continuing to trip and fall over other parts of the egoic self that still remain. Therefore, it is wise to continue our daily practice.

With Grace, this Quiet may stay within the forefront of our consciousness or it may recede. But if we are fortunate, this Grace will come forward into other aspects of our neurotic nature that are unnecessary and gently help them to release from our being. This space may even come forward and simply allow other aspects of our nature to be for now. Because of this deep allowing, our relationship to our egoic sense of self can deeply relax and there can be more room for us to be human, to make mistakes, and to fall on our faces; yet when we eventually hit the ground, we find it does not hurt nearly as much as it once did when we were so full of ourselves.

As our identification with our mind begins to dissolve and we live in this space of no-self more and more in an abiding way, we are moved by this greater force of Love. What begins to happen is that the experience of having no self or being radically empty becomes an effortless way of being. Living as emptiness requires no effort. There is no one there to protect or uphold an opinion, or desire things to be different. Imagine just how much effort is required for us to hold an opinion. As soon as we hold one opinion, we become cut off from or separated from all opposing opinions. Notice how it feels to dislike another political party than our own. We have to hold and maintain so many opinions, we have to put up a wall, we have to continue to look for reasons why they are wrong, and we have to continue to educate ourselves about why we are right. How much effort and pain does this cause us and our world? Imagine how much freedom and energy we would have if we did not do this. The invitation of "no self" is an invitation to step beyond our personal point of view and conditioning, into the freedom of no point of view, no conditioning.

After we let go of our agendas and our attachment to our personality as our self and allow ourselves to be taken and moved by Life, we no longer see life from our limited personal perspective. We lose the tunnel vision of ego and all of the reactions and defenses that go with it. There is no longer a fear of life—we have become one with life. We realize that what we are cannot be harmed. Our ego can be hurt and wounded if we believe in it as our identity. Yet what we discover through the dissolving of ourselves is that what we are is beyond our personal narrative or personal sense of self. We discover that what we are is beyond this lifetime and includes all lifetimes. In Reality, it includes all of Life; that is in fact what we become when the walls of our personal sense of self dissolve. We begin to live as the movement of Life Itself here on Earth. We become fully engaged with this work because all of our energies are in alignment with and not separate from the Divine. And, at the same time, we are effortlessly unattached in the world.

Practice: Self or No Self

1. Sit in meditation and simply observe the impersonal nature of thought. Notice how thoughts may *feel* personal, but ask yourself, "Is this thought my essential nature? What is my essential nature?" Experience this essential nature.

2. If you become again deluded by the feeling that thoughts are personal, ask yourself the following questions:

   - If something feels personal, does that mean it is so?

   - Who else could be having this same thought?

   - Do I know where my thoughts come from?

   - Do I know for certain that this thought is about me?

3. Again, step back into the space beyond thought and turn awareness upon itself. Turn awareness upon your essential nature. Rest here.

Philosophy vs. Direct Experience

For thousands of years, spiritual pundits and scholars have fought over the philosophy of self or no self. Traditionally, Buddhists have argued that there is no solid stable self within us—there is no "me" at the core of our being. The Yogic schools have argued that the Self is what we truly are. These philosophies and schools of thought have gone back and forth intellectually debating the nature of the self for literally thousands of years. But schools of thought are just that... schools of thought. Philosophies are just philosophies, and if we reduce our spiritual path to a mental activity, we will only become busier in our minds and no closer to Truth. It breaks my heart to see individuals waste their lives with such arguments when it is so obvious that both answers are true. The nature of truth is often a paradox of "both and" instead of "either or." Our minds are inherently dualistic and tend to become stuck in divisive viewpoints, and this is why so many of us spend so much of our lives in arguments. To come to know the truth is not a matter of the mind, but a matter of the heart. If we examine these deep spiritual questions from the depth of our hearts, we will ultimately discover our Divinity, the Divinity of this world, and their inherent non-division.

Unfortunately, most of us do not pursue truth from the open and vulnerable nature of our heart space; most of us pursue these deep questions from the analytical and defended space of our minds. I can remember being a freshman in college and taking a class on the development of religion and introduction to philosophy. By the end of the semester, my education had very rationally convinced me that God was a made-up idea and that we did not have souls. I had been taught two solid and rational arguments that clearly "proved" these points. But despite the logically crafted and clear arguments, my experience told me something quite different. My experience was that I have directly felt the Grace of God and I have directly experienced the depth of my soul. From a young age I knew that arguments can be true on paper, but in Reality—in our direct experience—we can know otherwise.

A mere rational argument does not actually mean anything in Reality; Life is not bound by our rules and logic. For the mature soul, this is common sense and we have long ago surrendered our will to this truth. For those of us who have not deeply contemplated this question, the realization that Life is the boss—*not us*—can upset our whole sense of how we view and interpret the world. If we examine how we come to imagine that reality works, we will notice that we employ our rational brain and intellect. But our rational arguments are just words strung together in a logical way. And after we have made our arguments, we then assume that we know how life works. But Reality is not logical; it does not have to follow any human rules, for it is beyond all rules and has its own intelligence which is beyond our understanding. What a shock this realization can be to our minds, which constantly try to figure life out. Our minds are so hopelessly looking for something to hold on to, trying to define this mysterious world so that they can create a perceived sense of safety. But Reality cannot be defined—it is beyond definition, no box can contain It.

Every argument we have is simply an insecure viewpoint, and every idea we have is less than the thing itself. God is greater than any idea we can ever have of God. We are greater than the ideas we have about ourselves. The only real way to know something is to become it and experience it firsthand, directly with no words or ideas separating us from the thing itself. We will never be satisfied to just read about or think about our True Nature, we want to experience it. What we are deeply interested in is the full experienced Truth of ourselves, of Reality, and to experience This as It runs through our veins.

When I reflect upon this age-old question of whether there is a self or no self, ultimately I find it does not make a difference. To be lost in our mind is to live in delusion; what is important is our direct experience, not how well we can argue or defend our egoic perspective. For years, I studied with two teachers who taught from these two different schools of thought: one taught that there was a Self and the other taught no self. This led me to experience much inner confusion. I found it unnerving to go see my teacher and listen to him say that there is no self when, in fact, I felt full of self. This experience challenged me to investigate for myself what my direct experience was. I read and examined both schools of thought, and I wondered how great Enlightened individuals could argue two completely different views of reality. Finally, after deeply investigating this within myself, it became obvious: both are true. When I look for a self, what I find is a collection of memories, various personality traits, hopes and fears, belief systems, and habitual ways of responding to life. Basically, I discovered my egoic personality. Yet there is nothing solid or tangible about the egoic personality. When someone argues that there is no self, what they mean is that there is no solid, tangible thing called a self within us. If we realize this, it lets the air out of our egoic balloon and our self-created egoic world collapses into itself, leaving only a spacious aware presence. If I were a scientist and tried to find a solid tangible self within any one of us, I could not find one. If I were a surgeon and tried to operate and remove the self, I never could. There is no solid self within us, this is true.

Our minds, however, fool us into thinking that the arising thoughts within us are who and what we are, and as a result, create the illusion of a permanent solid self. It fools us by constantly projecting thoughts onto the screen of our awareness. We mistakenly believe the projection of thoughts to be us—to be what we are. This is the great illusion. These projections are a movement of impersonal phenomena arising within us that we take personally *because* they arise within us. But if we examine this phenomenon, we find that all humans have the same phenomena arising within them—there is really nothing "personal" about these arising thoughts that we all share. Everyone more or less has the same movement of hopes, dreams, desires, and attachments. Being human is a universal experience, not an individual experience, although to our ego it certainly seems that way.

This impersonal self that arises within us is a mix of mysterious psychological forces, but no scientist has yet been able to explain it, extract it, or reproduce it. There is a movement of mind within all of us, which we assume *is* us, but if we look at this movement it is truly an incredible mystery. We do not know where our thoughts come from. We do not decide which thoughts arise within us. We do not decide or choose our wants, likes, desires, or our conditioning; all were given to us. Thoughts just arise, and as we identify with them and take them to be the truth of who we are, we ignorantly become them. This is the fundamental delusion. We believe the thoughts in our head and then unconsciously create an identity out of them.

But if thoughts simply arise within us, how can they be us? Would it not be more appropriate for us to say that we are the space in which thought arises? There is nothing stable, fixed, or solid about thought; it just comes and goes in a fleeting and impersonal fashion. Yet there is an active and vibrant space in which the thoughts arise, and this active, vibrant space does not come and go; this space of awareness is the one constant in our life.

From this direct investigation, we know three truths about our self: 1) We are the space that thoughts arise in. 2) We are aware. 3) This awareness is alive, vibrant, and intelligent. This all may sound very basic, but if we allow ourselves to see and experience these truths fully, we are in the doorway to our freedom. If we identify with and plant our feet in this spacious and alive awareness as ourselves, we are free. If we identify with the contents of our mind and their continuous movement, then we spend our lives unconsciously suffering, because we are at the mercy of the ups and downs of the impersonal nature of the thoughts which arise within us.

When we identify with spacious alive awareness, there is no suffering because there is no "one" here to suffer. The nature of spacious awareness is open, vast, alive, vibrant oneness. The nature of ego is separate, isolated, alone, desiring, and defensive. When we identify with spacious awareness as our self we become impersonal. Not many people like the idea of being impersonal. But being impersonal is our doorway to freedom. In a sense, if there is no me, then there is no one to suffer. The most self-centered individuals suffer the most in life. The most selfless individuals suffer the least, or if they do suffer, they suffer for selfless reasons. Being impersonal is the opposite of being egotistical. Ego is a movement toward self-centeredness. Being spacious alive awareness is a step out of self-centeredness and into spacious oneness. This shift of identity is a shift out of our self-centered egoic consciousness and into something huge and vast. Some may call this consciousness or the True Self. Some may call this "no self." But whatever we call it, no self or True Self, it does not make a difference. As long as there is a body, there will be some sense of self present. This sense of self will continue to have some conditioning, some preferences, some cultural influence, and a sense of individuality. If we did not have a sense of self, we would not know when to eat or how to operate in the world. And the less "me" there is, the less suffering will be present and the less suffering will be created in this world. The opposite is true as well—the more "me" we possess, the greater the opportunity for suffering, both personal and collective, because self-centeredness tends to create more suffering.

When we deeply let go of our personal me-ness, something much greater begins to take us over. We, as individuals, do not end up being nonexistent. What we find is that, after we let go of our attachment to the personal me, a Hugeness begins to inhabit us—our Divinity wakes up to Itself and begins to animate our being. Paradoxically, the first thing this Divinity does is actually love and allow for our humanity, the very thing we were trying to get rid of throughout our spiritual journey. As a result of this inclusion of our humanity within the space of our Divinity, we begin to be able to show up as a fully embodied human. How ironic is it that as we let go of ourselves we are more fully able to love and show up for ourselves and others? This whole journey is not about getting rid of ourselves, but fully embodying both our Divinity and our humanity and realizing that ultimately they both are one movement. From this space, the two worlds implode into each other and become one. This is the ultimate homecoming where we discover that no self and True self are one movement arising in the form of us.

Practice: Contemplate the Nature of Self

- How do you uphold or defend your personal egoic self?

- How do you experience your egoic self? How does it habitually manifest? Is it happy and joyous? Or does it center around suffering?

- What is the felt experience of letting go? What remains?

- How do you separate the world into human and Divine? Can you discover some ways they come together in Unity?

- What is your experience when you turn awareness upon itself?

~ Chapter Twenty-Eight ~

A Confidence in Our Divinity

A T SOME POINT ALONG THE WAY, WE DISCOVER a confidence in the innate goodness of life. We discover that no matter what our life circumstances are, this world is ultimately good, Love is greater than fear, and what we are is God Herself in human form. But to become this confident or this deeply and fiercely trusting, most of us have to have been beaten up a bit. It is like a boxer who gets in the ring... he knows that life hurts. He knows that sometimes he will win and sometimes he will lose. But ultimately, the boxer knows that he will be okay; otherwise he would never get into the ring again. To develop this depth of confidence, we have to get our hands dirty.

We have to be willing to have our heart broken again and again, until it breaks wide open and we remain free and open to all of life. To live life in this way takes a fearlessness and irrational—perhaps even insane—Trust in Life. This trust is not something that we have earned; it is given to us by Life as we openheartedly encounter what is difficult in us. At some point, after the rawness of life has ripped our hearts open for the last time, we discover that we are no longer able to hide behind the layers of egoic defenses that were once there. And so without those defenses we remain radically open. When we are open in this way, we feel and experience everything. We are no longer sheltered behind the walls of our egoic defense system. We stand naked before life as Life. As we discover ourselves as this radiant openness, we laugh because we realize that what we are essentially does not need to be defended, maintained, or controlled. And paradoxically, we realize that what we are is human, which means we feel and experience life through our human nervous system. As a result of this paradox, we discover we are Life Itself experiencing life in a human body at the same time, which means that we feel and experience all that arises. Sometimes this arising phenomenon is beautiful, wonderful, and blissful, and at other times it is absolutely painful. Yet despite the comings and goings of experience, we realize that we are the space in which all comes and goes, and so we remain totally untouched by it all. Simultaneously, if we identify with any of aspect of life, we will experience the feelings associated with identifying with what we think and feel. Our question then becomes, how fearlessly human are we willing to become? And can we include our life in all ways and on all levels, with love, as Love, even if that means not feeling good all the time?

At an early point along the path, I became very skilled in meditation. I made the commitment to sit every day for one to four hours and I developed a depth of confidence in relationship to my sitting practice. Nothing could shake this dedication to my practice. Inside me, a strength of character solidified around my relationship to my spiritual practice.

But Life pointed something out that I was missing, which was a huge shadow in my strength of character. Life pointed out that I had this strength in a very limited area of my life, but on a daily basis I was fairly proficient at living a completely divided and painful life, full of suffering and confusion. My relationships were falling apart, I was arrogant, I was stressed out and tense all the time, and I had no idea who I was. My dedication to my teacher, meditation, and retreat practice was amazing. But my strength, dedication, and willingness to fully show up to my practical life, were actually painfully weak. Life showed this to me repeatedly. However, I was really stubborn, so Life had to work very hard to get me to wake up, to embrace and include all of reality and not just limit my spiritual life to a teacher and a cushion. In my relationships with my partner, my children, my work, my dog, and the unpredictable nature of reality, I fell on my face again and again. This act of continually falling flat forced me to surrender to what Life was trying to tell me: Wake up, embrace everything, *I am everywhere and in everything*. Through this continuous surrender, a confidence and trust in the Divinity of life developed within me. That may sound paradoxical, but something happens when we surrender. We learn how life works. We see that there is something quite large that is in charge of the show and is not separate from the show. And that this something is not our egos... it is the Divine Herself. When we can see this Divinity everywhere—even in our pain and suffering—as the movement of Life itself coming to us in every moment, a trust in life begins to lead us, carry us, and become us. This trust grows out of the very things and experiences we fear. We start out with a fear of life, and as life beats us up again and again we notice that we have survived. We begin to trust that no matter what Life brings us, we will ultimately be okay, even if it feels like hell at the time.

Many individuals think that confidence comes from upholding or defending oneself through being assertive, aggressive, or dominating, or that it comes from constantly offering one's opinions, expectations, and desires. Many individuals strive to be the life of the party or the person with all the answers, or they strive to make the world dance for their personal needs. This is the confidence of the ego. But the confidence that I am speaking about is the knowledge that who and what we are cannot be broken—that we cannot be destroyed no matter what life brings us. As a therapist I have seen so many individuals who have experienced great pain and, as a result, developed a damaged mental outlook or very painful personality attributes. However, beyond this pain and woundedness, their essence remains pure, vibrant, and spacious. This purity of being is here despite all of the pain, suffering, and jadedness we have experienced. Everyone not only possesses this purity and goodness, but everyone *is* this Goodness.

Beyond the pain of life lies a deep Stillness and an undeniable Beauty. This comes as shock to many of us; we spend most of our lives so deeply identified with our pain that we cannot believe there is something quite beautiful underneath it all. This Beauty that I am speaking about is right here within us. This Beauty is our very nature. When we see this Beauty for the first time, we often cry. We cry because we know this Beauty is what we most essentially are, and we cry because it is so wonderful to finally come home to ourselves again. This recognition can be so shocking that many cannot accept this Beauty as themselves. And so they deny it and re-identify with their egoic nature, or project it onto a spiritual teacher, spiritual place, lover, or the experience of falling in love.

Even after we have given ourselves permission to be this Beauty that we are, we may fall into another trap: when our thinking mind comes forward again within the space of our consciousness, we may discount this Beauty as "just another temporary experience" that came and went. As we allow ourselves to get lost in our thoughts again, we quickly forget or ignore that this Beauty is here, everywhere and all the time, and that it is the very space out of which our thoughts arise. This Beauty that I am speaking about does not come and go. We simply cover it up or run back to our minds and old stories, giving our thoughts permission to define us once again because, for most of us, it is too uncomfortable and unfamiliar to live as the true brilliance of who we are. We do not want to live in such a raw and open way, but this raw and open space is where our Beauty lies, our true identity. If we are willing to know this Beauty as ourselves, we will gradually deepen in this.

This deepening also happens through life challenging us. If we can be challenged by life and reflect upon what remains beyond our emotional reactions and racing thoughts, we discover that our strength and our Beauty are here all the time. Life is always working for our growth, awakening, and evolution. We may get a glimpse of our essential nature while we are away on retreat. Then we come home and forget who we are once we re-engage in our busy lives. But as we examine how we lost ourselves again, we see that we chose to believe the thoughts in our mind instead of directly experiencing who we are. The invitation is that we choose to, once again, directly experience the truth of who and what we are. And so we do this over and over again until we can no longer be shaken out of ourselves, fooled by our minds and emotions. And humbly, we will find that, as humans, we will be fooled again and again. With humility we learn to surrender each day, even up until our own death. We learn to give up even our own idea of a perfect enlightenment. And we learn to give up the myth of enlightenment—that we will one day be unmovable like a stone Buddha. As we continue in a very humble way to surrender our humanity each and every day, we become free with the knowledge that, for as long as we are in form, our outward expression of this inward divinity can be always improved upon. As humans, we always have an evolutionary edge no matter how evolved we are; even the greatest among us can and do respond to life in an unconscious way. If we hold this attitude—that our outward expression will never be totally perfect—it will keep us honest and humble, and we will learn to continually surrender until our last breath. As we become comfortable with surrender, we become confident in our own innate Divinity and trust in the goodness of life, seeing both as inherently inseparable.

Practice: Divine Confidence

To develop confidence in your own Divinity, you need to directly experience yourself as Divine in each moment.

Begin by asking your own heart this question: *Who am I?* And then listen with your heart and feel the answer arise out of your heart. Listen and *feel* for what comes. Perhaps you will notice a sensation of warmth arise somewhere in your body, or a sense of Love or Divinity.

You can do this practice while driving your car, walking your dog, before you speak to another person, or even when you are in the middle of an argument.

The key to this practice is to feel into your heart and notice what arises when you sit deeply with the question, "Who am I?"

Practice: Mirrored Radiance

1. Stand before a mirror and look directly into your own eyes.

2. Notice the direct experience of Life pouring forth out of your eyes.

3. Notice the experience of Beauty that radiates from your eyes.

4. Notice the presence of what you are before a thought arises within your consciousness.

5. Be this Beauty. Be this Radiance.

For this practice to be powerful, you must be willing to *choose to be this presence* instead of choosing to be the habitual movement of your mind. As you practice this, you will become grounded in your presence as what you are, instead of being lost in the trance of your mind.

Practice: Surrender

Can you be so humble to not be right, to not know, and to not have the last say?

The desire to be right and to have the last say are far-reaching attempts of your mind to fill its insecure nature with a false sense of security based in "knowing." This illusory sense of security is false: all thoughts have no inherent reality; they are simply fleeting and have no substance.

To become intimate with what it means to surrender, you must *make your home in uncertainty* while noticing that uncertainty is okay. Uncertainty is the space of Life.

You can breathe in "I don't have to know" and breathe out "and I'm okay." Or you can breathe in "whatever happens" and breathe out "I am okay."

This breathing practice can be done anywhere; while changing your baby's diaper, in a meeting at work, lying down in bed, or even while someone is yelling at you.

Some time ago, a client came to my office and told me how angry he was with me. His anger escalated and he began to yell and scream. At first I tried to defend myself, but this only made him angrier. I then argued back, and he became even more angry. So I shut up and listened while his complaints went on and on. I knew his anger was not truly about me personally. So I sat there and I breathed in the heat of his anger and then I breathed out peace into the room, over and over again. When he was finished, I walked away with a smile on my face, armed with some colorful feedback about myself, and he walked away, relieved to have his complaints fully heard.

Whatever is happening in any moment, we can breathe in and breathe out. Sometimes it will be to breathe in "holy sh%#" and then breathe out "and that's okay." Sometimes we will breathe in our own hatred and sadness and anger, and then will we breathe out "and that's okay."

The disclaimer here is, of course, that we do not surrender to physical or emotional abuse or actual danger; in these moments we do what is wise: we leave, we call the police, we run, we fight back. However, when we are safe again, we have to also surrender that this experience, whatever it was, happened. As we surrender in this way, we become intimate with the places where we are insecure. We then have the opportunity to join with this insecurity—to jump into the very insecurity within us, into the groundless nature of life, and discover a spacious freedom. Within this insecurity we find a groundless security—an indestructible presence that is far different than the false sense of security that our defended egos offer us. As we give ourselves to this indestructible presence, what we become and how we relate to life is no longer moved by fear.

~ *Chapter Twenty-Nine* ~

Vigilance on the Path

I N THIS AGE OF SPIRITUAL MATERIALISM, WE MUST BE VIGILANT not to allow our quest to know God to become just another form of egoic entrapment. Each day may we offer this prayer:

God, may your highest will be done through me.

It is deeply important that we keep ourselves in the right perspective, lest we become both greedy and arrogant. Often, we must remind ourselves that this whole realm of spiritual awakening and liberation is not about us; it is not about our egoic nature waking up, or achieving something or some form of status, or having some experience. Spiritual awakening is about Spirit waking up to Itself, in us as Us. This Spirit is one with all of life. It is the very energy, force, and movement of Life. This is not a personal experience for our egoic nature to have. It is about the vast force of Divinity waking up in us and living through Us for Her cause and purpose.

To come into alignment with this movement, we must be humble, we must know who our Creator is—who the Boss is—and we must be willing to get out of the way, over and over again. We must allow the Divine to manifest Her highest through us until there no longer remains any division within us, between us and Her. Given our strong, persistent egoic nature, this full alignment may take a long, long time; our human manifestation will always be playing catch up with our inherent Divinity. This is the dance of being both human and Divine.

And so with humility we smile, we surrender, we let go and do whatever is necessary to come into alignment with Her movement. This is the path of Liberation; liberated from our ego, through humbly giving ourselves to Her will, again and again, until *Her and I* become one. This is our ongoing prayer and practice.

If we ever think there is an end to this dance of evolution, we are greatly mistaken. For as long as we are human, we are connected in countless ways to the collective consciousness of humanity, of our species, and that of this planet. Therefore, there is no end to this work. We can be humble and admit all the places within us where we harbor arrogance, greed, confusion, aggression, ignorance, specialness, and insanity. We can commit to transforming these unconscious forces in our lives and stepping into the Greater aspects of our divinity.

As we do this work within ourselves the entire world changes, for we are inextricably a part of one whole. This is our work. This is the work of the Yogi who is committed to the path of Liberation. Forever vigilant within ourselves and with our commitment, forever embracing our pain and confusion, forever surrendering our personal will and coming into alignment, forever growing, forever evolving, forever realizing our Divinity. Always being Buddha, always becoming Buddha.

About the Author

CRAIG HOLLIDAY IS A NONDUAL, HEART-CENTERED SPIRITUAL TEACHER and licensed therapist living in the mountains of Southwest Colorado. His work is dedicated to the discovery of our innate Divinity. He works in a way that addresses our everyday human suffering as a doorway to our inherent freedom. Craig offers Satsang, meditation classes, workshops, meditation retreats, and private sessions with individuals from all around the world online.

For more information about Craig, visit www.craigholliday.com.

If you enjoyed this book, please offer your review at the place of your purchase. Thank you!

Also by Craig Holliday:

Fully Human Fully Divine:
Awakening to our Innate Beauty through Embracing our Humanity

There is a value in seeing how spiritual awakening and being human meet in an ordinary Life, in relationship with our partners, kids, families and friends, with our busy lives, in illness, transitions, death, careers and in every area of our lives. This book is a call to awakening and embracing and transforming our humanity. It is a radical guide to spiritual awakening in the modern world.

Not written from the monastery or ashram, but from someone who has lived in the pain of samsara, from someone who after years of seeking and meditation found surrender in the depths of pain, while life was falling apart around him.

Available on Amazon in Kindle and paperback.

www.craigholliday.com